What Readers

"...the most intriguing book I've had the pleasure of reading, with lessons worth savoring. I could hear the words, see the sights, and smell the fragrances like no other book I have ever read. Truly incredible."
—Normie Kane, LCSW

"Really, really wonderful! A synthesis of spiritual philosophies that illuminate the human condition and bring fresh understanding. *A Hundred Ways To Sunday* offers hope that my struggles really do have a purpose."
—Jean Perkins, Artist

"Brilliant! Robin Rice has opened the doors to the ancient, spiritual, shamanic realms, inspiring hope, love and courage for anyone who wants to personally grow and make a difference in this world."
—Rose Khalsa, Director of The Shaman's Circle

"A fast-paced story of wisdom and intrigue to touch your heart and soul. The more I read, the more I was hooked!"
—Stacey Wolf, author of *Stacey Wolf's Psychic Living*

"I couldn't put it down. There were parts that were so familiar and others that felt like I was in class learning from a great teacher. I am still reeling."
—Pam Fields, Realtor

"A delightful journey of discovery and self-understanding. It works its way into your imagination, your thoughts, and your life."
—Paul Shaw, Economist

"A truly brilliant book. It set me dreaming again."
—Tamela Tilly, Business Administrator

A
HUNDRED
WAYS
TO
SUNDAY

ROBIN RICE

BE
WHO
YOU
ARE

Published by
Be Who You Are Press
P.O. Box 57
Riva, Maryland, 21140

www.BeWhoYouAre.com

Printed in the United States of America

Cover Design by Dotti Albertine
Author Photo by Jennifer R. Amrine
Book Design by Jonathan Gullery

Rice, Robin D.
    A hundred ways to Sunday / by Robin Rice. -- 1st ed.
    p. cm.
    LCCN 2001117473
    ISBN 0-9710876-4-4

    1. Spirituality--Fiction. 2. Shamans--Fiction.
3. New Age movement--Fiction. Goddess religion--
Fiction. 5. Reincarnation--Fiction. I. Title.

PS3568.I2943H86 2001   813'.6
                                     QBI01-700567

In Memory Of
Nelle Bouterse and Ricky Rice

&

Dedicated To
My Awesome and Amazing Children,
Richard and Taylor

Acknowledgements

A project of this scope is never undertaken alone.

My first and greatest thanks must go to Terry Nebeker, who listened as I read aloud for two years, laughed every time I said "I quit!" and reminded me again and again I could rise to the challenge of my task. She also worked on preparing the manuscript for publication, offering valuable advice at every step in the process. Her assistance is evidence that behind every successful woman there is at least one more.

I want to acknowledge Loree Lough and Cindy Whitesel, who began teaching me to write fiction long before this book was begun. Because of their time and expertise, I had the tools in which to tell Mary's story.

Thank you to my spiritual and shamanic teachers, especially John Perkins and the Amazon shamans, and other writers including Debbie Ford (*The Dark Side of The Light Chasers*), Arnold Mindell (*The Shaman's Body*) and Dennis William Hauck (*The Emerald Tablet*).

I thank Daniel and Leander at Canyon de Chelly Tours and Timothy at Thunderbird Lodge for their wisdom and guidance in the canyon. (This is a good place to point out that every character is based on a composite of many other people I have known and no character is based on any one particular person. Also, while the essence of this story is true, the events did not take place in Canyon de Chelly. As such, please forgive any misrepresentation of Navajo legends, traditions, culture or people.)

My very special thanks goes to Suzanne Brinks for sharing the story of her father's death and her own experience of taking flight to the edge of the Other Side with him. Chapter 35 is dedicated to them both.

I also want to thank my first readers and editors, Rosemarie Brown, Bob Drews, Pam Fields, Tamela Tilly, Karen Geiselhart, Leah Hinkle, Normie Kane, Rose Khalsa and Paul Shaw.

Finally, I thank my children, Richard and Taylor, for teaching me that every person, no matter what the age, has soul-knowledge that is worth listening to. It is because of them that Puck is all that he is in this story, and I am all that I am as a human being.

A
HUNDRED
WAYS
TO
SUNDAY

1

Oya, the nine-headed goddess of tumultuous change, stared at me all that first night. Actually, I was the one staring at her, given she was nothing more than a hand-carved block of African wood. But it felt like she was staring back, even more like she was trying to say something. Since I have only one head and it is skeptical of anything supposedly divine, I couldn't make out a damn word.

I did notice, though, that she was not wrapped in anything remotely African, but instead a help wanted section of an Arizona newspaper. I also noticed a huge coffee stain next to a job as a bookmobile driver on a Navajo Indian reservation.

Of course, a coffee stain alone would not have done it for me. But I'd ordered the statue when I was in Nigeria years before, and I've spent my career studying indigenous shamans from around the world. Was it mere coincidence she arrived on the very day I had been turned down for funding on a project that would have allowed me to begin studying Native American shamans?

On the other hand, I have no great affinity for Oya. I don't even know much about her beyond a notorious reputation for tornadoes and windstorms. I just thought she looked cool enough to add to all the other statues I've collected over the years. So, maybe it was a sign from the goddess, and maybe I just needed a job. Whatever the case, that's what got me here, waiting for Jimmy Two Feathers in a trading post that looks like a cross between a cheesy five-and-dime and a sacred burial ground. That, and the desperate hope that all the other bizarre coincidences that have been littering my life for the past ten years are actually leading somewhere.

Jimmy knows I'm here. The RV outside is a dead giveaway.

As usual, he's making me wait. I finger the weave of a small, three-hundred dollar rug I'd love to purchase but have no place to keep, silently sending a greeting to the three Navajo Yeí spirits woven into the fabric. I get no discernible reply.

Any time now, Jimmy.

I don't mind the wait, really. It reconfirms what I've been suspecting these past six weeks—that there is something going on here worth knowing about. Jimmy makes it pretty obvious. Always slinking around when I come in, speaking in a guttural, horsy kind of whisper, his eyes shifting like he's making sure no one sees us doing business. It's kind of strange, because around everyone else he's a hyper-friendly salesman who knows how to get even the thinnest wallet open.

At first, I thought he must have thought I was up to something covert, as if my bookmobile was really a cover for some governmental spy ring sent in from D.C., which I did mention was my hometown that first day we met. Or, like most of the Navajo out here, maybe he was just wary of tall, independent women who travel around in uninvited, oversized RVs.

I don't think it's either of those things anymore, though I can't yet say what I think it is. In the end, it doesn't matter. I play along, shifting my eyes and roughing up my whisper, because Jimmy's got the best quartz crystal you've ever seen. And if I have a true love, it's quartz. I'm even working on my slinking, though I doubt I'll pull it off. I'm a straight shooter by nature, and thus far, whenever I've tried to add a little mystery to my gait, I've just looked like I had one of my beloved rocks in my shoe.

I'm pretty sure he sees through my efforts anyway. Deep inside the trader's heart, there's a hard-as-granite spiritual wisdom you don't find in every man out here, no matter how pure his tribal blood. I can see these kinds of things. Just like you can't kid a kidder, you can't *not* see a seer.

Now that I think of it, maybe the slinking routine is a game we both play so we can pretend we don't see what we do in each other. The idea sends a shiver down my spine and a cold energy racing along the bottom of my veins. It makes breathing harder and everything I see begins to appear more vivid, as if alive.

I know this feeling. I had to feel it a dozen times, just before unexpectedly meeting some revered shaman or spiritual guru, before I would finally admit there was a reliable connection. But then, some of us like our epiphanies to fit neatly into rational, reasonable little boxes, even when they pertain to what I like to call the Great Mystery. In short, some of us are slow learners.

I hear the dull swish of the heavy rug door that separates Jimmy's private quarters from the back room of the store and look up to see his stubby, leather-like hands carefully unwrapping something that resembles a small fireplace log. By the shake of his hand I'd gauge it weighs at least a few pounds. No way this is what I ordered.

"I asked for hematite," I whisper, going for the horsy sound.

"Wait," he grunts, fumbling with the bright, multi-colored cloth wrapping. His lips are pursed and his heavy eyebrows furrowed, making his fifty-some years look like more.

"Hematite," I repeat. "You know, little smooth drops of silvery stone, looks like dark, solidified mercury?"

No response. I wait as he fumbles.

"How much?" I finally ask, knowing whatever the price, it's likely to cost me more than the hematite. Jimmy could out-con even Raj, the best Asian jeweler I know. Raj could bait and switch faster than you could take one sip of the orange soda he insisted you enjoy as his honored guest.

"Wait," he grunts again, though I get the sense he's taking his time on purpose, getting some kind of dramatic mileage out of the mystery.

Serves me right. I didn't really need the hematite. I only wanted an excuse to get back in here, where the action is.

I wait, reminding myself it's not so much the extra money Jimmy is after, but the joy of the hunt. His true delight is in the kill of the cash register. You can see it on his face, just below the surface if you are looking, every time the antique machine dings and thrusts itself open. It gets downright obvious when his new credit card machine gets a swipe. Pure delight pushes past a mouth full of tooth decay.

"I'm not paying more than..." I start to argue, but at last the prize is unveiled. My jaw drops and the rest of my words won't budge.

We both look in silence.

"Where the hell did you get this?" I finally demand. I try to keep a clean mouth out here, my way of appeasing the Navajo elders who are kind enough to let a white woman roll a gas-guzzling monster up and down their sacred land day after day. But I forget more often than not.

Jimmy says nothing.

"This isn't what I ordered," I say, stating the obvious.

"You like it," he says with a sly smile.

Like it? Shimmering shards of soft opaque stone, in a huge, nearly transparent slab that pulsates with vitality. I've never seen a piece of selenite so lovely.

But more than the actual slab is what went into getting it. Jimmy has a way of knowing what stone I am going to ask for next, especially if it is one I dreamed of the night before. All last night this very slab had danced in front of what the New Agers over in Sedona would call my third eye. It was singing to me, like a lover cries for the beloved long gone. One might say it was just a dream. But before coming to the reservation, I was never one to dream. Not even as a kid.

I try to eye him directly to let him know I know something funny is going on. A true Navajo, he avoids my gaze.

"Forty-nine, ninety-five," he offers.

Fifty bucks. High for selenite, but peanuts for the magic I feel leaping around my gut.

"Where'd you get it?" I ask, reaching for a casual tone. I want to know who is listening in on my dreams, or maybe even sending them to me. My intuition tells me, as it has before, that it's someone other than Jimmy.

"A Chief," he replies.

Bingo!

My head jerks upward. This time I succeed in locking his eyes.

"What Chief?" I nearly yell.

The volume startles him. He looks away and shrugs, like it's no big deal. But it is overdone, giving away the truth. It is a big deal. A really big deal.

"What Chief?" I repeat, this time softer and with a forced smile.

"Let the selenite tell you," he replies, pushing the stone toward me.

I lose the smile and take the slab. Slivers too soft to penetrate the skin flake off in my hands. It sends me reeling, threatening my balance. Magic.

As if from a distance, I hear Jimmy repeat his offer.

"Yes," I reply, too awed to bargain, too caught up in what dreams may come next, not to mention when and how I will meet this Chief.

"Hell yes."

2

"Mary Margaret Hathaway," Eric says slowly, holding me at arm's length after a long hug and seductive once-over. "You don't look a day over twenty-five."

That's Eric for you—still thinking flattery will get him anywhere. Why not? He's the one who doesn't look over a quarter century, when we're both ten years past it. Flattery probably still gets him most everything he wants, like it always did in college. That, and the millions he has floating around, even after three divorces.

He blips the alarm to his European convertible, puts his arm around my shoulder and starts walking me toward my bookmobile. I nearly stumble in the fancy shoes I keep tucked away for special occasions. Today hardly qualifies as a special occasion, but it has more potential than any other event in the last half year, and I've got to remind myself I'm a woman every now and then somehow.

"I really appreciate your taking the time to show me around," he says. "I want the new shop to be loaded with real Indian artifacts, but I wouldn't know a genuine article from a Made-In-China teepee. When I heard you were out this way, I thought, what a perfect excuse to see you and get a little..." he hesitates, raises his eyebrows in innuendo, "consulting."

He stops and stands back to look me over again. "When did you get so pretty?" There is a dripping sincerity in his voice. "I mean, you always did look good. Nearly six feet," he reaches out to touch my hair as I pull back, "with those dark curls and magic blue eyes."

I roll my eyes in the most unmagic way I can muster.

"Now that you've put on a few pounds," he continues, as if I asked for his updated assessment, "you don't look so scrawny and lanky. In fact, a little makeup and you'd have the men howling at the moon out here."

I shake my head, unable to process all the backhanded compliments at once. I'm tempted to tell him that the last thing a little makeup will do is get the men howling at the moon over me, given that the Navajo put makeup only on their dead. He's trying so hard, I don't have the heart.

"Cut the crap," I say. I'm more than willing to help him sort his plastic teepees, but I'm going to draw the line hard and fast when it comes to my personal attributes going up on his chopping block.

He offers an exaggerated sigh. "Mary, Mary. You never could take a compliment. Is it so hard to believe I find you pretty? We were lovers once, you know."

"Once" is the key word here, pal.

The only reason I've agreed to see him again is because bringing a paying customer to the Two Feathers Trading Post is a perfect way to win brownie points with Jimmy. In my mind, I bring Jimmy a customer buying in bulk and he tells me where I can find this Chief. Easy trade, though Eric obviously has other ideas.

To be honest, I was a bit curious about what might happen between us myself. People can change over the years after all, and it's been a long time since I've had any intimate companionship. One look at him getting out of his perfectly polished car, though, and I knew it hadn't been that long. It's not that I disdain flashy millionaires. I just know better than to think we have anything in common.

"Thanks for the compliment," I say with a flat smile.

He smiles back, then puts his hands in his pockets, as if satisfied to have made some headway. "So how's the bookmobile business?" he asks as he climbs into the passenger seat. He's a good six-four, but it still seems to swallow him.

I give a fatalistic shrug, unimpressed with my forty-foot monster, ironically dubbed by its maker as the Ultimate Advantage.

"What's the problem? Isn't it all free, like a library?"

I sigh and shrug again, trying to decide if I want to go into it all. Better offer the condensed version.

"The Navajo Nation never asked for a white woman with a fancy degree to drive books around their reservation in a huge RV. Especially one funded by a rich white pompous ass who thinks he knows what a proper education is."

"So that 'Master's In Generics' is really paying off," he jests, grinning as he gets in his digs about my studying sociology instead of taking his advice to get a "real" degree in something like business or law all those years ago.

I don't bother to mention that I've now studied shamans from fourteen tribes in five different countries and completed everything but my dissertation for my Ph.D. Why, when despite twenty-six boxes of research, I can't seem to get a damn word written?

"I assume the whole project will be nixed any day," I add. "In fact, I can't imagine why it hasn't been already."

Eric grunts a laugh. "They'll boot you off just for trying to help?"

"It's all right," I reply, not wanting the Navajo to be blamed. "The white man is still too quick to run over indigenous people with our own ideas of what constitutes an education."

Truth is, if I had known what I was getting into, I would never have taken the job. Which is probably why that information wasn't revealed to me in the first place.

"It's not what I think I'm here for, anyway," I add softly, almost to myself, then instantly regret it.

"Uh-oh, here it comes," my companion jests, grinning really wide now, showing off his large, perfectly straight teeth.

I drive in silence, a statement more than punishment, only now realizing how much I want to tell someone what really is going on. But who would understand, when even I don't? And what is there to tell? That shamans from every part of the world have divined for me a destiny beyond any I'd have dreamed of for myself? That each one then simply blessed me and sent me on my way? That again and again I have been left so desperate to put the pieces together that I'd follow clues like bread crumbs, all the while wondering if it wasn't just some ego-centered hoax? Who would believe what I couldn't believe myself most of the time? Certainly not Eric.

"I'm sorry," he backpedals, sounding genuine. "Tell me

what you think you're really here for. I want to know." He leans toward me, looking at me so intently you'd actually think he was interested. I wonder if that is part of his gig now, to get his hooks in deeper. Probably something he learned in a Fortune 500 seminar. "You still want to save the world, right?"

I take in a full breath and exhale slowly. So, he did know me. A little anyway. The idea of being known, truly known, by anyone sets off a pang in my heart. It is something that lives in me, like a lost hope I can't remember, no matter how hard I try. I look at Eric, considering an honest answer.

No. Best keep it light with the likes of him.

"All the world that I can," I reply with a pasted on beauty-queen smile, then lean over with a nudge to his ribs and add, "which I'll lay odds doesn't include you."

"I'm beyond saving." His voice is low and soft, surprising me. I can tell he believes it. It makes me lower my defenses long enough to really feel for him.

"Nobody's beyond saving," I offer, "unless they think they are."

"Like I said...," he answers forlornly, now looking out the window.

I look with him at the glorious sun-baked landscape of ruddy golds, pale yellows, and muted greens. Though I have traveled this road hundreds of times, I am still in awe of the giant red mesa in the distance. Struck afresh by the early morning light, it seems to eagerly await each new inch of the sun's illumination. The scent of sage and sandy earth is evident, even after being filtered through the air conditioner. I'm grateful. There is nothing like a good whiff of Arizona to bring you to your senses.

I am tempted to suggest that Eric take a long look and an even deeper breath, to point out that the land is alive out here. Mother Earth is willing to communicate if we are willing to learn a new language. I resist the temptation. She can speak for herself. Certainly her natural inspiration is far more capable of working a miracle for him than I am.

We drive in silence, past the mysterious, nature-carved hole in the stone landscape that gives the town of Window Rock its name. At last, we turn onto the half-mile dirt drive

that leads to the Two Feathers Trading Post. My breath quick-
ens and my heart nearly hurts from excitement. It's been a long
time between gurus.

"So," Eric says, "is this Feathers guy a haggler, or is it best
to just go with whatever wholesale he'll offer?"

"You two were made for each other," I reply, then park and
jump down from the RV. I imagine them having at it over a few
dozen handmade turtle rattles. Yet I know who will suffer most
if Eric keeps pushing for a rock-bottom price.

"Haggling is expected," I add. "But try to remember that it's
not just Jimmy you have to consider. Indian craftsmen and
women will use their portion of the earnings to eat this winter,
so be as generous as you can."

He looks at me like I'm from outer space. Again, I feel the
pain of witnessing a life without meaning. Yet the notion
instantly draws me up short. What am I thinking? Eric's life
has as much meaning as mine. I'm as big a fool as my boss,
thinking I know better what another man needs. Besides, my
way has hardly gotten me where I want to go. Who am I to
preach?

I walk into the shop with my head bowed in self-recrimination. Not two steps in the door, I trip over Jimmy's elderly
mother, known to the tourists as The Sandwich Lady, toppling
her and scattering her goods on the floor.

"Aaaeeeee," the short, rounded woman squeals, her bright
purple skirt hiked up, revealing knobby, well-aged knees.

"Ah, shit," I whisper to myself.

3

"I'm so sorry—I didn't see you," I offer, fussing profusely, though I know Jimmy's mother doesn't speak a word of English beyond her one line of "Sandwich, egg and bacon, mutton and cheese, one dollar." Her tortilla breakfasts, each tightly wrapped in a piece of tin foil and a napkin, are a favorite among natives and tourists alike.

"Aaaee, Aaaee," she yells in pain, glaring at me. She stands, then begins testing her foot with her weight. The cooler she carries has opened and several of the sandwiches have been flung across Jimmy's dusty floor.

"Eric," I command without looking at him, "buy the ones on the floor. Make it look like you really need that many."

To my surprise, he quickly falls into action, putting on his charismatic smile while assessing the damage. He puts out his ten fingers and says "Sandwich?"

The woman nods after glaring at me again, not fooled for a moment. He picks up the foil packages, counts ten—nine from the floor and one from the cooler—and goes for his wallet. Jimmy makes his way toward the commotion.

"Mutton and cheese," The Sandwich Lady says in a heavy native accent, pointing to several of them with a permanent marker slash, "egg and bacon," she points to the others marked with a circle, "one dollar." It's obvious she's in pain, but I know her sale is more important to her. Her pride, too, no doubt.

Shit. Shit. Shit.

He gives her a ten. The woman stands tall and proudly flattens her skirt. With a final angry look to me, then to her son, she limps off.

Eric unwraps the foil of one of the egg and bacon tortillas and takes a bite. "Hey, these are good."

"She cooks with her soul," I say, wondering why today of all days she has to show up so early. It is usually noon before she arrives at this shop.

"It was an accident," Eric assures.

It is nice of him to say, but the idea offers no comfort. Knowing me, I'll instant-replay the whole incident for days. Good old Catholic guilt. Enough of it in childhood makes total renunciation later in life nigh impossible.

"Too bad," Jimmy says, looking at me like I was the one who had been hurt.

"I feel terrible." Selfishly, the feeling is not only for her. How am I going to get Jimmy to tell me anything when I've just run down his mother?

"She will be fine," Jimmy replies without emotion. "You? I'm not so sure."

"This is a friend from Phoenix," I tell Jimmy, quickly pulling out what ought to have been my trump card, now just hoping to break even. "He wants authentic Native American crafts to sell in a new shop he is opening. I told him you were the man to see."

Jimmy grins and nods repeatedly. "I can get you everything you need. My people make the finest you will see anywhere on the reservation. One-stop shopping!"

Eric smiles and shoots me a knowing look.

I nod once, trying to be glad for him.

"First, I must talk to the lady," Jimmy says, surprising me.

My heart beat had begun to settle, but this sets it roaring again. He pulls me to the back room, then ignores me to put some finishing touches on a box he is readying for the mail.

Just like a Navajo, playing it close to the vest even when they want to talk. Or so I've come to conclude. Six weeks out here and most of what I know I've learned from the children's books on the bookmobile and a few weaving women I saw years ago at a Smithsonian program back home. I won't let myself read the other books. I like to learn first-hand about a tribe, getting to know them for who they are today, before I read how the historians have chosen to remember them. Problem is, the Navajo don't seem to want to be known, at least not by me.

Jimmy's gestures are wide, drawing attention to what he is doing, as if he wants me to see without having to speak of it.

He lifts a handmade drum from the box. A mere six inches tall and some twenty inches around, it is made of tightly pulled deerskin, with ancient symbols that make your eyes cross to look at them. They are deeply soaked into the hide, more like a huge tattoo than a paint job. Looking at me, he bangs the drum once to declare its stunning, deep resonation, then nestles it gently into its wrappings again.

The sound sends a chill up my spine and sets me rocking from heel to toe. I'll bet a month of my dismal pay this drum is important, or will be.

Jimmy scrawls the address at an angle perfect for my viewing. I pay attention, which seems to satisfy him. He addresses it to Mary Margaret Begaye on Juniper Street in Scottsdale, with the return marked "Wyunetta Morningstar" in care of the shop. None of it means anything to me, beyond the recipient having my own first two names.

"Is this what you brought me in here for?" I ask.

Jimmy doesn't look up. "My mother. You gotta catch up to her."

"Do you think she needs a doctor?"

He waves off my concern. "The Chief has sent for you. She knows him. That's why she was here early. She knew you were coming."

"Damn!" I say, mumbling a second, internal "damn" for forgetting my language with him yet again. "Why didn't you tell me out there?"

Jimmy shifts his eyes. "Your friend. He is not like you. He is not a part of the plan."

"And I am?" My breath is getting harder to control. A plan? Jimmy has never said anything like this before. It's like, suddenly, I'm in the loop.

"Go after her. She will not want to help now. She will see this as a bad sign." Jimmy willingly looks me in the eye, a shocking gesture. In his eyes, I see he is speaking in earnest. It is almost as if he is somehow rooting for me.

"You must prove to her that you are The One," he says, putting the package on a shelf behind him.

"The One to what?" I ask, frantic. My mind races to cover the details. What am I going to do with Eric? And the book-mobile?

Jimmy does not answer. It doesn't matter. I rush back to the main area of the store where my companion is picking up cheap toy drums with seeds on either side, batting out a puny beat.

"These are fun," he says.

"I have to go," I reply, breathless. "You can drive the RV, can't you?" I pull out the keys and shove them in his hand, knowing that if I can drive the monster, anyone can.

"What? You can't be serious."

"I'm really sorry. It's important. Leave it in the parking lot where we met. I'll get it somehow."

"Well, uh, wait..." He stalls while I shake like a jumping bean. "I don't want you to get stranded. Why don't you take my cell phone? Call me when you want me to pick you up."

Through the window I see my guide getting farther and farther away. I can't think straight. "It could take days," I say.

He smiles at me warmly. "Then it takes days. This seems important."

"It is." I take the phone, more to keep him happy than because I have any intention of using it. He follows me toward the door.

"Thank you," I offer, surprising myself by hugging him.

"Hey," he says, pulling back but keeping a hand on each shoulder. "I'm just a dumb jock on a shopping trip. But I know one kind of genuine article when I see it. If anyone can save the world, Mary, it's you."

The unexpected support touches me, but I see the old woman has made it beyond the drive, now limping only a little. I give Eric's arm a quick squeeze and take off, only to run smack dab into Jimmy again. Will my every step be thwarted?

"Find the one who is lost, my sister," he says in a solemn voice. "We cannot live without faith."

The one who is lost? Who is that? The Chief? But then how could he be asking for me? My urgency leaves me unable to think. The only thing I know for sure is my guide is getting away. I bob my head in agreement to whatever it is Jimmy is asking of me.

"Now go!" he urges gruffly.

I bolt out. Halfway down the long drive, my side aches. I want to call out for Jimmy's mother to wait up, but realize I don't know her name. I don't even know Jimmy's real last name. It's not like I can just yell out "Hey, Sandwich Lady," or "Wait up Mrs. Two Feathers!"

Ah, well, name or no name, it doesn't matter. My destiny is hobbling up ahead of me, finally in clear sight. There's no way I'm turning back now.

4

Three hours later, the Sandwich Lady's cooler is finally spent of food and I have lost my purse. It is no doubt in one of the two dozen shops we visited. But I have no idea which one. What's worse, my guide still appears to have no more intention of acknowledging my presence than she did when we first started hurrying down dirt roads, beating our feet into stretches of paved highway and pummeling heavily weeded paths. I look down at my feet, swollen in my shoes. Again I curse my vanity for having worn pretty but uncomfortable shoes today instead of my usual hiking boots. All on the off chance I might want to impress an old lover.

I look with pure envy at my guide's moccasins as they pad her along her route. Less desirable is her native costume. Her bright red shirt of crushed velvet is long-sleeved and tucked under a satin purple skirt. It is belted with a six-inch strap of leather that is heavily studded with huge pieces of silver and turquoise. The bead and coin-like ornamentation around her neck also seems a burden in the dry heat. A little fancy on an average day, even for the women elders. I wonder if the Chief has anything to do with this, or if it simply helps sell sandwiches to the tourists. Then again, perhaps it just makes her happy.

I sigh under my breath as we continue on, careful not to upset her in any way. The natives along her route were careful not speak to me after her warning nod in my direction, though one brave soul whispered that her name is Wyunetta Morningstar. It took me only a moment to make the connection to the drum in Jimmy's shop.

So, I know her name, that she knows someone with my first two names, and that she has superb taste in gifts. I've been trying to guess her age. Probably late seventies, given that Jimmy is in his mid-fifties, though I wouldn't swear by either assessment. Hard work and the elements can age a person out here, faster than you might think.

It is more information than I had three hours ago, but not enough to help me. What am I going to say? "Hey, Wyunetta, Respected Elder, what's all this about some Chief wanting to meet me?" No, all I can do is wait until she's punished me sufficiently and keep up with her until then.

The only thing that keeps me from turning around to try and find my purse and make a pick-up call to Eric is that, angry as she is, she hasn't stopped and looked at me in wonder as to why I'm tagging along. She knows that I know. And she knows that I know she knows. It's a dance, to be sure. I will hobble along it if it kills me.

Having passed through a short distance of wooded area, we come upon a clearing and a hogan. Good timing, assuming she lets me in. A storm is brewing in the distance. They come fast and furious in the heat of the season, often causing flash floods in the low-lying areas. Already the sky has darkened.

We approach the six-sided hut, a circular formation of un-peeled logs built to symbolize the geometric structure of the Navajo cosmos, as I learned at the Window Rock museum. Most of the Diné, as the Navajo call themselves, have at least one traditional hogan, even if they also have a white man's style house on the property. Here, there isn't a modern convenience in sight.

Smoke swirls from the center of the roof in a steady stream, perfuming the entire clearing with the scent of well-cooked meat and heavy spice. As I consider the implications, a sense of dread grabs at my empty stomach. Inside, lunch could be cooking. Not a bad thing in and of itself, but lunch to sell to the whole Navajo Nation, like breakfast? And what about dinner? Might we have another six to eight hours of selling before the day is done? My feet pulse with pain, but there is self-flagellation on its heels. Why should my Great Quest be easy, when such an old woman's day-to-day life might be so hard?

"Humph," I grunt to myself.

"Humph," the woman repeats.

Oh, hell, my grunt was overheard. No doubt my hostess will take it the wrong way. I look up to see arresting, elderly brown eyes waiting to look into mine.

I am tempted to avert my gaze to retain my soul's anonymity. But no. Such cowardice will get me nowhere. I consciously plead to the woman's dark orbs. To my surprise, they grow in majesty as we connect, seeming to me like a bottomless maternal lake.

Mercy is all I am asking for, I say wordlessly. Mercy to find the Chief who seeks me. To understand what everyone wants of me, and maybe find what I am looking for, too.

"Humph," she grunts again, turning to walk through the hinged door.

I don't know if I should follow or not. Her gnarled brown hand keeps the door open a few seconds longer than if she'd just walked in and let it close behind her, so I take a chance.

Inside my first inhabited hogan, I breathe in the heavenly aroma and let my eyes adjust to the dark. There are windows with the curtains drawn, plus smaller panes placed around the smoke hole at the center of the ceiling. The dirt floor is broom-swept nearly as tidy as tile. Moist air from the boiling pots rise in a steady stream, bringing me to a profound awareness of my hunger, both for food and something else, too. A home, maybe, though the thought is an unusual one for me.

Mostly, I am content to be a traveler. I've never had much use for staying in one place, given my difficult childhood, and no real reason to settle down since. A place like this, though, has an atmosphere so rich you know it will become a lasting memory. It could tug at a person, make her wish she was the belonging type.

"You don't look like The One to me," I hear a man say from the far side of the hogan. The deep, angry voice startles me, jump-starting my adrenaline. I grab the leather pouch that hangs by a leather string around my neck, ever ready to give me a boost of power. Or so my shaman friend Maria from the Amazon promised when she gave it to me. Placebo or not, it works.

I strain to make out the figure. A red light the size of half a dime glows deep and then deeper. Behind it, a male face. I keep looking until my eyes fully adjust. I see he is slumped over, sitting on a cot shoved tight against the wall. The smoke of his cigarette swirls out in oblong O's, like little ghosts.

Without warning, Wyunetta starts ranting at the man in her native tongue while she goes around lighting a few oil-burning lamps. The man, thirty years old or so, makes no move in response. She rants again until he bitches something back.

The disrespect of any elder sets me off. It's more than that, though. Something else. Something wrong, like their tones are laced with hate. Not the kind of resentment that comes and goes between family. That is understood. More, it seems like a dangerous hate. A feudal hate, if you ask me to tack intuition on to my guess. I shudder involuntarily.

"The One what?" I ask snidely, feeling petty and justified at the same time. I'm certain, though I can't say why, that in allowing this tone, I have also begun some kind of war with this stranger. Despite the warmth of the room, my hands grow cold. Not a good sign.

He stands. "The One to save us all," he replies, extending his arms awkwardly, like a vulture's wings, to mock me further. The gesture reminds me that in Egypt, the vulture is considered sacred because it can eat death and not die. I can't say I like the vision that conjures up right about now.

"I don't know anything about that," I say stiffly, though Jimmy had said the same thing.

Before he can reply, Wyunetta is loudly shooing him out with a broom. He moves slowly, in his own good time. I want to warn her, tell her to be careful. This one is dangerous. Instead, I hold my breath, willing him past the door, past the moment when he might turn and snap her broom in two, or worse. He opens the door, spitting slime between his legs, then goes.

"Oh lovely," I say in low tones, "he chews and smokes at the same time. Long life to you, buddy."

She shuts the door just as the rain begins to pelt down. I watch her as she returns to busy herself with cooking. I am greatly relieved, yet she seems even more so, her mood suddenly lighter.

In the silence, I am given too much time to ponder. How is it that everyone out here seems to know who I am supposed to be, when I don't have a clue? How could I be this "One" anyway? I'm a white woman. And who is it Jimmy says I am to find, this person who has caused some loss of faith? Like a match lighting the matchbox, these new questions ignite so many of my other, well-worn ones.

Will I have a chance to change even the smallest part of the world for the better? What if I don't? Or what if I do get the chance, and fail? How will I justify my existence? Who will I be, and what could drive me to wake up in the morning, if in the end I'm nothing more than an average Catholic girl with delusions of grandeur? Why is it such things plague me, when others seem content to live life without asking such deep questions? Why do the shamans say I am someone important in this world, when I have almost nothing to show for my existence? What is this future I have been chosen for? And who is it that has chosen me, anyway?

The questions, and the many years they have gone unanswered, make me tired. I look up from my internal self-torture to see my hostess watching me with a kind of gentle pity. She offers a nearly toothless smile that seems genuine. My heart feels a surge of something grand, though I cannot begin to say what.

The winds howl around us as the rain thrashes the hogan. Paying no mind, Wyunetta offers me a taste of her stew. There is an apology in her every gesture. I have no idea what has turned her around. But I accept, happily.

"Good," I say. "Very good."

Wyunetta slaps her knee and lets out a cackle as the lightning strikes.

I look at her, grinning. Who cares if the rains come? Here, for this moment, I am safe.

5

I have to be completely upfront here. I'm a baby mystic, if I deserve to be called even that. True, I've done buckets and buckets of research on shamanic spiritual practices and the effects they have on the social systems of the tribes they serve. Careful only to observe, I've nonetheless picked up a few tricks from the various medicine men and women I've encountered. But I don't pretend to understand how this "knowing" stuff all works, or why. Or why it does sometimes and not others. At minimum, I know that my own faith and practice, or lack of them, get in the way. So when I say I want to save the world, it doesn't mean I know what I'm saving it from, or to, or that I have any clue how I'm going to do it. It's just not that clear to me.

Nor do I have any idea what's changed Wyunetta's tune. But from the moment the smoking, chewing jerk walked out the door, everything shifted. She went from an angry, offended old hag to the mother of all mothers, warm and nurturing, as if her one and only joy was to make sure of my comfort. The meal, prepared for me alone, was five-star indigenous dining. The moccasins she provided, steeped in sympathy and warm herbs for my blistered heels, came only after she'd finished a downright divine foot massage. All the while she smiled, often cackling at some inside joke, as if she had the most honored guest in all the world in her home. I have no idea what to make of it.

Every so often she touches my face tenderly. Tears come to her eyes as she shakes her head. Whatever it is she thinks she has found in me, it is precious to her. I'm honored, even though I don't get it. I have tried to use hand gestures to ask her questions, but she only nods and looks to the door, as if we are waiting for someone and that will explain it all. Perhaps the Chief?

A knock at the door brings me front and center with my nervous excitement. The door opens. It is a young Navajo girl, shy and demure with a dirt-smudged, pudgy face. She's no more than ten by the looks of her. The rains left us an hour ago at least, but she looks as if she were caught in it, then sun-dried. She wears a simple skirt, a blue T-shirt that shows a cow being roped, touting the local rodeo, and black, hightop sneakers that seem a little too big.

Though I am disappointed, Wyunetta seems to have found just what she has been waiting for. The old woman speaks rapidly in Navajo to the child, who nods in rhythm to her words, looking between the two of us at regular intervals.

"Welcome," she says formally, a little stiff, as if she's done this translating before and is not overly fond of the task. "This is your home. Do you know it?"

"Thank you," I say, unsure exactly whether she is asking if I know I am welcome, or that this is to be my home for a while, or what. I hesitate to say more, not wanting to risk offending Wyunetta again. However wonderful she is acting now, I have not forgotten that her mood can turn on a dime. With my apti-tude for screwing up, I could easily lose all the ground I have gained with one wrong move. My feet are healing, but they are in no shape to walk off any more offenses.

"I am grateful for her welcome," I say, bowing slightly with my palms pressed together in front of me, a habit left over from my days in Tibet. "Please tell her lunch was wonderful."

The girl complies. Wyunetta smiles at me so wide, her whole face squishes up. Only the eyes, sparkling and alive, show the youth still inside her. It charms and confuses me. Can this be the woman who cursed me so vehemently with those same eyes just hours ago? Her face clouds over for a moment, as if my face has given my thoughts away.

She speaks again. The girl listens.

I lean forward, tilting my ear toward her voice, as if hear-ing better might make me understand more.

"She says this morning she did not believe you were The One, because you pushed her down. She did not think The

One would do that."

The girl stops to listen for more. Again I want to apologize, to tell her it was an accident, but I don't want to interrupt. The girl nods to Wyunetta and turns to me. "She says you argued here in her hogan with the man we call Dark Crow. He was here to test you to make sure it was really you. Now she will lead you to Chief."

I let out a long breath, unaware until now of holding it. A thousand questions run through my mind. Like why would the Navajo call anyone in their tribe by a negative name like Dark Crow? But first things first.

"What would she like me to call her?" I ask.

The girl asks my question.

"What you feel to call her," she says, then looks to me as if to ask if I understand.

I hadn't thought about what I would "feel" like calling her, but immediately my thought is Great Mother. "I would call her Great Mother, if she allows me."

To this, Wyunetta bends at the knees, slapping each one with an open hand, nearly doubling over in happy shrieks, then hugging me, again and again.

Once she calms, I return to the child. "Will you ask her about this Chief for me?" I'm thrilled for the attention, but I need to get to the heart of why I am here. "What does he want with me?"

Great Mother's face sobers at the question. She speaks with what sounds like great precision. I feel she is intent that the translation be exact.

"She says she will point the direction, but you have to find him on your own. Dark Crow will drive you to Canyon de Chelly in his truck tonight. That is his agreement. You will be safe for this journey only. After that, you must avoid him. He is dangerous to you. Do not forget this."

Like I need to be reminded. That guy's dangerous to society.

"You must enter the canyon and go deep inside, past where anyone lives. You will have guidance."

Great Mother speaks while I reel at the thought of riding nearly two hours with the jerk they call Dark Crow, without a purse, without Eric's cell phone, without Great Mother to lead the way.

Just as scary is de Chelly. I've been to a scenic overlook once. A beautiful spot, magical even, from afar. But when I considered going in, I stopped for fear it would be ominously filled with the ghostly energy of natives cornered and killed by the whites. Not to mention the Anasazi, or "ancient aliens" as the Navajo call them, who high-tailed it out of there for no apparent reason five hundred years ago. I shudder.

Shoving the thought from my mind, only to have the image replaced by the fear of skin walkers. The fear was instilled in me by a few Navajo who warned of certain stretches of highway I might not want to take at night. The Navajo version of modern-day voodoo witches, the skinwalkers wear animal skins to take on the power of the animal, casting deadly hexes on anyone they don't like. The Indians out here are firm believers, so much so they will jump out of their seat at the mere mention of it. Wouldn't the overgrown nooks and crannies of de Chelly be a perfect place for such evil to crouch and hide, ready to pounce?

My mind continues to whirl.

Even if there are no ghosts or skinwalkers, the mass of rock could send a sensitive like me reeling with an overdose of its energy. I nearly passed out in the Grand Canyon. De Chelly is smaller, but that only means the high walls are closer together. I get dizzy just thinking about it.

And then there are the lions and bears that make even the Navajo elders wary of going in for fear they won't be able to move quickly enough should one pop out from the bushes.

And wild dogs.

And the dreaded Navajo trickster, the coyote.

And quicksand.

Holy shit, I am so in over my head.

Great Mother speaks over my fears, then allows the translation. "Your Great Mother says to not be afraid. Your task is important, so the Holy People will lay out your path."

My mind searches furiously for any argument that will stand against that kind of proclamation. I latch on to the idea that no one but the Navajo are allowed to enter de Chelly without a guide, but give it up before speaking. Spiritual quests leave no room for such cowardice. Anyway, it's not like I haven't faced the wilderness on my own before. I've just never liked it.

I notice that Great Mother's eyes have welled up again. She begins to speak in a voice that is choked. In response to her words, the girl's eyes fly open wide.

"She says...she says...she has waited a lifetime for you who once...." The child's face flushes, contorted as she fumbles for the words, "drank from her...you know."

I shake my head and shrug.

In exasperation, she tries again. "Drank from her...." She can't say it. Instead, she awkwardly points to the old woman's sagging breasts and runs out of the hogan, the door slamming on its hinges.

What? Wait!

I look to the direction she has flown, confused. A thousand thoughts ram through my brain before I can settle on the obvious. Great Mother thinks she has breast-fed me?

That's crazy.

How can she think I am her daughter? I'm as white as we whites come. Does she think she was my nursemaid? She's too old for that. Besides, I'm from the East Coast. And I was bottle-fed like every good Catholic girl. No, I am quite sure I've never seen Wyunetta Morningstar before in my life.

Dread overcomes me.

I'd say they were insane, or up to something, but my hostess is too serious, her actions too heartfelt. Jimmy, too, called me "sister" in great earnest. However untrue, these people must believe it.

A new reality hits, a truth that feels all too familiar. Another dead end. Another round of hope, vanished, like the child out the door. The Divine Trickster once again playing with my life. Assuming there is a Divine Anything out there.

I stare at the door, as though answers might magically appear. None do. Only one thing is for sure. I'm not who they are after. Not The One they think I am. I'm a stranger after all, and only that. My heart pumps heavily as a deep sadness settles in the pit of my gut. I am unsure what to do with my disappointment, or Wyunetta's when she finds out. Selfishly, mine is the one I grieve for. It's over. My quest is no closer to completion than it was in the RV with Eric early this morning. Looking into Great Mother's eyes, I feel that I will miss her. She did not turn on me. It was the gods. Again.

Enough. I must bring myself to tell her of this mistake. Jimmy, too, must be informed. But how? I find myself racing to the door to look for my translator. I need help to explain so that I can bow out gracefully, without offending or disappointing anyone too much. The girl is gone. Sunshine pours in through the door, mocking me. I turn back inside, to the home that, for a brief moment, was opened wide to welcome me.

Only now do I realize the truth. I would have gladly faced Canyon de Chelly, alone, with all its terrors, not to feel this way.

6

I hadn't planned on taking this ride. What I had planned on was telling Dark Crow that there had been a mistake. I was not The One they were looking for. I had assumed Mr. Hostility would be delighted with the news, only too happy to explain everything for me. I figured Wyunetta could get word to this Chief guy without my further involvement. I'd be free to go find my purse, call Eric and get back to my bookmobile. From there I would decide what to do with the rest of my life.

Dark Crow, showing up at the first signs of dusk, just laughed at my objections. "Tell Chief," he said from the window of his beat-up flatbed, not bothering to get out.

After Wyunetta railed at him about something, he sniped back and told me to "just get the fuck in." Out of respect for Wyunetta, I did as told without a caustic reply. Before I shut the door, the woman who had treated me like a daughter all afternoon handed me a backpack stuffed with a few Navajo shirts and skirts, plus my shoes. I had watched her pack and tried to protest, explaining for the hundredth time that I really was not who she was looking for. I'm pretty sure she thought I was only protesting the gifts, since she would not hear of my refusal.

So, now I am traveling to Canyon de Chelly with Dark Crow's hard jaw set in some kind of protest of his own. He's driving in a perpetually hostile silence along back roads I don't know. My only consolation, now that the rain has passed, is that as a passenger, I can fully enjoy the beauty of the magenta landscape as sunset nears.

Actually, "enjoy" is too strong a word. The truck's interior makes true enjoyment impossible. It has a thick layer of smoky film and grime covering every inch, save where fingerprints have smudged it off. This is no doubt due to the lack of a window crank on my side and any interest by the driver to use his.

The one long seat we share bounces with the drive, making a creaking sound that irritates. It is torn at the vinyl seams. Cigarette burns scar the thinning fabric. One rip, a little nearer to Dark Crow than me, is the length of the seat from back to front, revealing dirty, tired foam. It is such a clean split, I can't be sure if it occurred from normal wear and tear, or if Dark Crow created it in some fit of rage with the hunting knife he wears at his side.

The thought gives me visions I don't want to see. Imaginations only, I hope. I won't forget the warning that this is the only trip I'm to take with Dark Crow. Not that you could pay me to take another. I again look at the rip and consider the wisdom of even this journey. If I'm not The One, which I have foolishly confessed to my driver, all bets on this guy's willingness to get me where I'm going may be off.

So, we have back roads, a knife, and a woman alone with a terminally angry male stranger.

Calm yourself, Mary Margaret.

Okay, well, I suppose it is logical that a native would take the back roads. I know a knife is not uncommon out here—as standard issue as a rifle. And angry Indian males are plentiful enough on the reservation. Most are just good guys in a difficult situation. Few have the ugly negativity I sense in my driver. Anyway, due to some kind of agreement, he is taking me to a Chief. Some kind of respect must come with the task.

That means I'm probably safe. Most likely. I exhale raggedly.

The road goes on and the silence becomes a standoff. I'm not going to talk. Neither is Dark Crow. He looks at me directly every so often, checking me out without trying to hide it. To keep looking like I'm totally fine with our situation, I look back in like fashion.

He's twenty-nine, thirty maybe, a few inches taller than I stand, which is pretty tall for a Navajo. His strong native face has harsher than usual features, so maybe he's only part Navajo. It might have been a handsome face, were there a hint of kindness, or even humor, to it.

His hair is long and jet black, pulled back into a pony tail, though obviously not to keep it tidy. It reminds me of a real horse's tail. I can't imagine it's seen a brush in under a year. I imagine lifting it up and finding a real horse's ass underneath. The thought makes me laugh to myself, a small smile eking out, though I sense it's a dangerous allowance.

At least *I* have a sense of humor. It helps me endure his dirty, long fingernails and those awful teeth, which show in the awkward way he opens his lips into a square when he lights a cigarette. They are a band of yellow with spots of black between several of the front ones. Seems the guy is averse to all kinds of brushes. Enough to make you shudder.

His red T-shirt is void of comment save some weird symbol I don't recognize and his black jeans are a little too tight. Big Man On Campus, yeah buddy. I try to imagine this "look" seducing a woman, or even some young Indian girl looking for a boyfriend. I can't. I simply cannot picture this man making love to anyone, though his taking a fist to a woman's face is a readily available image.

In fact, I can see a cheekbone shattering at the impact. My own cheek heats up. It is the kind of reaction that often happens to me during an unexpected vision. I hope it is not me at the receiving end, but then, would I wish it on some other woman, maybe some young girl, someone not as strong as I am? I send a silent prayer that if it has to be someone, let it be the strongest among us.

Big Man On Campus clears his throat with a nasty sound and opens his door to spit as we fly down the dusty road. I'm tempted to open my own and vomit. Instead, I turn my thoughts to better men. This Chief, perhaps.

I wonder if there is some angle I might take to get my driver talking about him. I know little beyond his interest in putting rocks and gems into my dreams. Am I to look for a huge headdress and war paint? Does he live somewhere along the beaten path, or tucked away in some alcove a lifelong native would have trouble finding? I can think of no angle that allows me to save face in my silent spar, except the old adage about losing the battle to win the war. It will have to do.

"Do you know this Chief?" I ask casually.

Crow-boy turns to look at me full on, like I'm an idiot to think he's going to talk to me, let alone tell me anything I want to know. Just when I am sure he's not even considering giving me an answer, he speaks up.

"I owe him. Waited a lot of years to pay up. Now we'll be even."

Not the kind of answer I was looking for. But I like knowing more about this agreement Wyunetta also mentioned. Delivering me to this Chief is something Dark Crow wants to do, has been waiting to do, to pay off a debt, which means I probably am safe. I feel a knot in my right shoulder release a bit. I rotate my arm a little to help it along.

"What did he do for you?" I ask, trying to make it sound like it's no big deal, just an idea of something we might converse about.

My driver looks at me again, eyes boring into me, like I'm stupid.

I wait it out, get nothing, then try another approach. "What do you know about him?"

"Nope," he says, not looking, then gets a little sick kind of smile that shows more teeth than I want to see. "Too much fun keepin' you worried."

"I'm not worried," I say, a little too defensively. "I've been in the presence of some of the greatest men and women in the world. I'm just curious if this Chief guy is going to be someone I want to add to that list. Or if he's nothing more than another average guru who thinks he's something special. I've seen those, too."

I impress myself with this impromptu bait. Dark Crow doesn't take it, but I can see he's thinking about Chief, about whether he is or is not something special. He shifts in his seat, seemingly uncomfortable with his own mental wanderings. I like this idea, too. Flat out, I can tell you that Dark Crow is not one of the good guys. How bad he is, whether he is actually following evil on purpose, or still just blindly lashing out from his own hurt like most of humanity, I am not sure. But nobody's going to put a white hat on this cowboy.

"What places you been?" he asks. Something in his voice

catches my attention. I hear a vulnerability, a wanderlust with a hint of envy. He's probably never been anywhere.

"All over," I say, shrugging. "Twenty-six countries, last count, but a lot of them were in Europe, where you can travel into and out of a country in an afternoon."

He thinks on that for a minute.

"What's the worst thing you ever saw?" he finally asks.

I look at him squarely, assessing that I'll be given a moment or two to think about it. It's an interesting question, one I've managed to avoid asking myself. My mind reviews the train stations in Old Delhi, where so many people live on mats of filth that you can't walk to your train without hurting someone. Then there are the ten-year-old prostitutes in Haiti, little girls who have never been little girls. Or the peace-loving Tibetan nuns who no longer feel worthy to wear their orange and saffron robes because they have been repeatedly and brutally raped in Chinese prisons. And in Calcutta, there are seven-year-old boys who carry twenty pounds of mortar on their heads every day from sunup to sundown, not even knowing what a school is. How does one choose from such equally worthy options?

"I've seen worse than you, I bet," Dark Crow says to my silence. I realize he asked the question not so much to hear my answer, but to have an excuse to give me his own.

It doesn't matter. We are at war. I'll use anything he gives me. Like a stalker, I wait, stone-faced, a grin in my heart.

Strategy is everything.

7

"What have you seen?" I almost add "Dark Crow" to make it sound like I'm being genuinely attentive. I quickly consider that this is not likely the name he prefers to go by, if he even knows that's what the others call him. Since I've never been properly introduced, I leave my question as is.

He smiles in a cockeyed way, as if he wants to impress me with his callousness.

Yeah, Whoever-You-Really-Are, I see right through you.

It makes me feel good to prepare, just as the martial artist prepares, for confrontation. Let your opponent's own force be his downfall by moving out of the way at the last minute. This is a classic opportunity.

"Saw a man get his heart tore out by a bear, way back in de Chelly, where you're goin'. Arms and legs ripped up, too, like he's nothing more than a cooked chicken pulled apart."

I wince.

Dark Crow waits for more, seeming to want a bigger reaction. "His kid was watchin'," he adds, leaning in toward me like he knows this part will get to me. "Was too scared to scream. Thought the bear might go after him, too."

I can picture it in my mind all too vividly. It catches me off guard. The father, the son. It grips at my heart, as if the panic were mine. Any thought of using such an image for ammunition in a psych war, even with the likes of Dark Crow, seems irreverent, if not downright wrong.

"That is a terrible thing to see," I say.

I look at him for a response, but none comes. For a moment I imagine he was the kid. I feel the first inklings of compassion for him. What if it was Dark Crow that watched his father and the bear? I can imagine how that might have made him like he is today. The more I go into my seeing place, the more my right shoulder knots, and the more I feel it is true.

"Were you the son?" I ask in a soft probe. This I would never use against him. This I would use to help him, if I could. Maybe he needs to talk about it.

"Fuck, no!" he replies loudly, again looking at me like I'm a dumb white bitch.

Instantly, it pisses me off to have even considered caring. My heart snaps shut. "Well then just what DID happen to turn you into such a perpetual sunshine factory?"

"Nothin'," he says, looking all the more disgusted with me. "There's nothin' on the Rez to make you nothin'."

Well, well. So that is it. As impossible as it seems, I have found something in Dark Crow I can relate to. Nothin'.

If I know about anything, I know about Nothin'. I know how Nothin' can break you. It's a slow break, never as clean as one you can point to. The truth is, I can work with any Somethin' that happens to me. But there is a certain Nothin' that is happening, has been happening forever it seems, that I have no idea how to work with.

Suddenly Dark Crow looks like a mirror image of me. The thought sends my shoulder into a full-blown spasm. I grab at the tight pain, a long-time ailment that flares up at the choicest of moments.

It's tempting to try to share the thought with him, to explain that we are more alike than we are different. But it wouldn't work. No doubt he's as certain that I have every choice in the world as I am that he has at least some.

We drive in silence until he slowly pulls over to the side of the road. Though my eyes had been adjusting as we drove into the night, I realize it is finally fully dark. My driver has not turned on his headlights.

Here it comes.

My mouth is suddenly as dry as the desert we are swallowed up in.

"We'll sleep here," he says curtly. "There's a blanket in the back. Or..." his voice takes on a hint of seduction, "you can stay up here with me." I can barely see his lips smiling, yet his yellow teeth seem to glow in the dark. I shudder involuntarily.

"We can't be more than an hour away," I argue, speaking logic in a cracking voice.

Damn it, girl, show no fear. No. Fear.

"Headlights are out," he says, the smile now in his voice.

Cat and mouse, I realize, trying to breathe. He's winning.

"You knew you didn't have any headlights before starting a two-hour drive at nearly dusk?" This realization pisses me off, moving me beyond my fear enough to appear strong. We are in the middle of nowhere. My blood drops a few degrees, racing erratically through my veins.

"Had one when we started," he replies, music in his tone, "I thought."

I don't believe him. It makes me mad enough to think straight for a few precious seconds. I grab Wyunetta's pack, get out, slam the door, and go to the back. I can hear Dark Crow laughing. It is a cruel laugh, one that delights in winning by a large margin.

The floor bed is a ripple of dirty metal, still wet in the bevels from the rain. The heavily soaked blanket looks like it was made by Mexicans, not the Navajo. This angers me even further. Not that I have anything against the Mexicans. It's just that I think he ought to have more loyalty to his own. I put on both extra shirts and skirts in my pack and pull the blanket over me, thankful I can't see what it might be infested with. Safety in layers, God hope.

"Idiot," I say, louder than I intended, finding a sliver of bravery in the window that separates me from my nemesis. Again the laughter.

An old tire serves as my pillow, with the pack to soften it a bit. The angle will undoubtedly put a huge mother of a crook in my neck. I force myself to think of Old Delhi and the train station layered with the homeless who sleep in far worse than this every night. That usually works when I find myself in especially unpleasant circumstances. Tonight it doesn't.

Only two things comfort me. The moccasins Wyunetta gave me, worn and soft, healing me as I massage my feet through the leather and fur. And the Arizona night sky, a mixture of silk and velvet, dotted bountifully with silvery-white stars.

It reminds me of what Ita, a Peruvian jungle guru once said to me after telling me she was not the teacher I was looking for. "The night is our explanation for all pain and suffering. Without the darkness of night, the stars cannot shine and the morning cannot come. Do not only wait for the morning. Find value in the night. Then you will know God."

The idea of knowing God, which I do not presume in any way, offers some comfort, though I don't believe, after all these years, that I can gain enlightenment in one night. In the silence, I hear Dark Crow's breathing change. I feel his energy shift to sleep, for the moment, anyway.

Relaxing a bit, I press my thumb hard into my shoulder where it hurts most and try to understand this fiasco. I get nowhere.

Cut your losses and look forward.

On to Plan B: Tell this Chief I'm not who he thinks I am, see if he has any insight into who I really might be, and then ask him if he can point me further down my path. There always seems to be such a wise one when I am most desperate, when I am most likely to throw in the towel and try to be like other people with a house, a car, and a steady job. The thought usually makes me ill, but tonight, with a tire for a pillow, it has a certain appeal.

I shift my weight, imagining the bruises I'll pick up from the hard waffled floor beneath me, not to mention the chafing from the watered-down blanket.

Damn it, I do this too often. I forgive the Universe, or whatever gods and goddesses run it, too easily. Especially after leading me down another blind alley. I take the bread crumbs like a mouse and tell myself to be grateful for even that.

Why I do this is beyond me. I guess I just can't help it. I've always found hope where there is none. Eric once said I could find positive symbolism in a noose, especially if things were bad enough for me to be coming across one. He was right, but what's the alternative? What have we, if not hope? Besides, a noose doesn't have to mean death. It can mean death of the old way of life, a prelude to the phoenix rising.

Or so I comfort myself. One day, though, I may have to admit I'm as delusional as those who find warmth and meaning at Thanksgiving dinners where everyone argues the whole time.

I look up at the moon, a few days shy of full. It reminds me of a card game I used to play as a kid at our torturous yearly family reunions. What was the name of it? I can't even recall now, but I do remember that I always liked the part where you could risk everything to Shoot The Moon. The idea was to get all the bad cards, all the wrong cards, all the cards that would kill you if you were trying for a good hand—the very cards nobody else wanted. If you succeeded in getting every last card, you won big, hitting the jackpot of jackpots.

I remember what it felt like when I had all but one of the deathly cards. Praying that the bad would add up to something worth it all, as afraid of a good card coming along to ruin your plan as everyone else was of the very darkness you held in your hand. I feel something like that now. It doesn't quite fit, but it's close and I'm beat.

"Amen," I whisper, leaving the rest blank on the off chance the Powers-That-Be have any idea of what it is I ought to be praying for. God knows I don't.

8

Dark Crow starts the engine, squealing onto the road before I am fully awake. No doubt it is his way of putting me in my place, making me ride in the back without so much as a bang on the window between us to say we're going. When I finally come to my senses, I feel my body to be sure that I'm really here, really alive.

Yep. I have made it through the night. I have not been raped or even nudged throughout the half-slept hours. This Chief must have some real sway with my driver.

I smile and take a full breath. This kind of morning, with golden sunshine streaming through the trees, lighting up the sandy earth, is the kind in which I cannot be rattled. I even prefer it here in the back of the truck, out in the early morning wind, away from Dark Crow's vulture-like energy, not to mention his smoke and spit.

I take off my extra clothes, stuff them in my pack, then lodge myself into a corner. My body aches at the hips and ribs, but my spirit is high, a surge of hope that on many mornings I am unable to avoid no matter what the circumstances. I wonder at it often. It's as though it's in my nature to be glad whenever beauty shines her holy face upon me, at least until the day wears on. I look around and breathe in deeply again and again.

Despite the turmoil of the Navajos, and the hell of a history this land has seen, the reservation is a good place to believe in some kind of God, or gods. The colors are striking—glittering gold, burnt orange, hearty red, subdued yellow, sandy brown. They appear in combinations that change every hour until sunset, which brings a whole new backdrop of striking pinks, muted purples and majestic blues. Each new bend in the road is proof positive of miracles, if you're the believing sort. If not, it will at least make you wonder if Mother Earth hasn't carved herself on purpose, bulging out in one direction and sucking in another, a yang and yin of her very own divine breath.

I've considered all the major religions, in a grazing kind of way, but nothing rings truer than what I see this very morning. Only in such untouched patches of earth does her stunning elegance line the roads, free of charge. True, a few street signs show man's official influence. But here on the reservation, even these tell of hope. As if to confirm my thoughts, we pass a road sign that declares Mr. and Mrs. Tony Wallerman have adopted a stretch of the road, committing to keep it clean. Anywhere else in America, it's a corporation, thinking of the advertising opportunity. Here it is Tony and his wife, loving the land. It makes me believe once again in all things good.

A bird above is following so high up I can't make out its species. Like the bird, I feel myself rise to look down on myself. Being the Witness, as the enlightened ones would say. This flight has long been my only meditation practice, my only relief to free me of me when the hell of life comes crashing down. Today, as ever, it offers peace.

So what if Mary Margaret Hathaway is not The One? The One for what? Something in the future. Yet the future does not exist before I get there. I laugh at myself, at the worry I had yesterday to not be The One for a future that does not yet exist. When today, now, I am. I simply am. I laugh again, using Mary Margaret's hand to reach out and catch the wind in delight.

Suddenly, the truck jerks, as if it has hit something. My head bangs against the cab, reeling in the bird that I am, returning me to Mary Margaret's body with a thud. Dark Crow pounds on the window as we come to an abrupt halt.

"Get in," he hollers out his slightly opened door, then spits.

"I'm fine here," I yell back.

I wait. Wait more.

It's no use. He won't drive until I have come up front.

The reason for all this commotion comes into my knowing without effort. Dark Crow wanted me to feel insulted, but I was laughing. Winning on the only level that really matters. My joy was killing him. Feeling generous enough to resist rubbing it in, I climb into the cab, silent, but still happy. No one can steal your joy—I remember a wise woman from Jamaica once saying—only you can give it away.

Inside the cab, his fury is as palpable as my happiness. He takes off, spinning his tires into the dirt, leaving a dust so thick I cannot see behind us. Yet my mood cannot be disturbed. Here, now, I am outside of his energy and influence. Let him be whoever he wants. I am. I smile, unable to help myself.

"You are fuckin' crazy," he accuses, throwing the words like darts that don't even hit the board, let alone the bull's eye.

I answer him in genuine question, allowing the sing-song in my voice to ring clear. "Do you hate me because I'm white, or because your people think I'm The One, or what?"

"I don't fuckin' hate you. I don't nothin' you. You're nothin' to think twice about," he says, adding a look that says much the same.

"Oh yes, that Nothin' again," I say with a hint of a jeer. "Nothin' to make you Nothin' on the Rez, isn't that right? Now Nothin' to make you think twice about me. That Nothin' is pretty powerful stuff with you."

"Shut the fuck up," he says, his eyes narrowing.

I've hit a nerve, but I can't help myself. I push. This is a guy who needs to face himself, or be lost forever. Or so I judge from my side of the truck. "Yep, Nothin' has you by the balls. Nothin' to do, Nothin' to care about, Nothin' to look forward to."

In a flash his knife has gone from the side of his jeans to a few inches from my throat. "I said shut the fuck up!"

I haven't hit a nerve, I've hit an artery—the source of his lifelong misery. I'm surprised by the knife, yet not. Part of me leaves my body, calm as you please, to become the bird. I must have known this was coming.

I watch the scene with a detachment I can hardly believe. I feel myself take a sharp breath but keep looking at his face. I avoid looking at the knife directly, though the me that is still here is acutely aware of each bump in the road as we hit it. One big pothole and I'm a bird forever.

Yet in my heart of hearts, I just don't think today is the day I am going to die. Like a fool, I keep pushing.

"Go ahead, kill me now," I say, like I really don't care. "Put me out of my misery."

Suddenly, surprisingly, I am deeply in touch with that. My misery. The hell I go through, my own version of Nothin'. I am the bird, hope and misery, all at once. It seems clear, clearer than clear, as I watch from my bird self. I wonder, is there any way for me to keep this clarity? Am I in that near-death place I've heard of, seeing not my life, but my lack of understanding, pass before my eyes? How I wish I could capture the lessons as cleanly as I see them right now.

At the same time, I am deeply present with Dark Crow and his need for something, anything I might have to give. I am fascinated by my own generosity. Or do I think I owe him something?

"You're not miserable," he accuses. "You're fuckin' happy. Fuckin' laughing, like there's something to laugh about in this fuckin' place."

My mind is razor sharp. It finds my voice, eager to express. "It's a fine line for anyone, buddy. You'd know that if you got off the reservation long enough to look."

I pause for reaction. There is none. He's not stopping me from telling the truth anymore. Probably because he knows he can stop me completely with a short thrust of his wrist if I go too far.

"You want to know the worst thing I ever saw?" I continue boldly, as if it is I who have the knife at his throat. "Nothin'. I've been all over the world and I found so many people drowning in Nothin' I cried until there were no more tears left in me. Your Nothin' comes a dime a dozen, cowboy. I have a heaping shitload of it myself. So don't think you've been specially picked to suffer. Nobody's that special."

As if divinely planned, we approach a main road. Dark Crow looks at the cars coming from his left, then his right. I can see him considering. In the end, it appears his street smarts prevail. He slides his knife back into its cover.

We ride in silence, but it is a new silence. The hate has cleared, at least for the moment, which gives us both time to ponder the truth I have spoken.

Soon enough, I see the signs for Thunderbird Lodge,

which rests at the mouth of Canyon de Chelly. My life and sense of self have been spared another day. But for what? For wild animals and skinwalkers? Not to mention a mistaken Chief I must correct, and whatever consequence that entails.

You do know how to get into it, girl.

We pull up to the parking lot and stop so abruptly I am forced to grab the grimy dashboard to keep from flying through the windshield. As if to have yet another last word, or perhaps even issue a warning that this war has only just begun, Dark Crow turns toward me and blows a cloud of cigarette smoke in my face.

9

The good thing about staying overnight in Dark Crow's truck is that here, at the Thunderbird Lodge, there is a twice-daily jeep tour I can take deep into the canyon. If I'm lucky, it will drop me at Chief's door. I'll have a few hours to explain things to him, then the afternoon tour can pick me up for my return. I'll be out of here by dinnertime, on my way back to Window Rock and life as I have known it for the past six weeks. After the fiasco with Dark Crow, it has far more appeal than it would have a day ago.

I ask about the tour at the gift shop desk. Nelson is the name of the next driver heading out. He's going as far as they go, to Spider Rock, several miles in. I go outside and see him, with his clipboard in hand, already loading people onto his massive twenty-passenger, open-air vehicle. The going rate for the tour, as the woman at the desk made clear when she looked at my pack and wrinkled appearance, was forty dollars. For half a second, I was tempted to explain that I had no money on me, but an elder had told me that the path would be laid out before me by the Holy People. The woman's set face told me she wasn't too interested in anything beyond her forty bucks and maybe a smoke break. I have a hunch the driver might know this Chief, so I decide to approach him directly.

"Are you Nelson?" I ask, even though I've already heard him introduce himself half a dozen times to his passengers.

"That's me," he replies, extending his hand with a tour guide's paid enthusiasm. He has a wide smile with heavy crow's feet on a fat face. I like the way he wears his cowboy hat, as if it is an old friend. I take his hand and his expression changes, his crow's feet digging in deeper, his smile now warm in a real way.

"You're looking for Chief," he says in a thick Navajo accent. A statement, not a question.

Bingo again!

"How did you know?"

"He described you. Told me you were coming. Here's your purse."

Like magic, he pulls my purse out from under his front seat. My jaw drops. A bit grease-stained, but here nonetheless. Impossible.

I take it, immediately tempted to see what's still there. I think twice, not wanting him to take this as a kind of unspoken suspicion that something might be missing. I put the strap over my shoulder.

He smiles and nods once, as if knowing my thoughts and satisfied with my decision. Another seer?

"Thanks, a lot," I manage. "How did you get it?"

"Someone found it. Took it to the radio station in Window Rock. Someone who seen you with Wyunetta Morningstar said it was yours. She said you were on your way here. Leroy Chee was coming this way so he brought it last night." A frown creases his forehead. "We were a little worried it took you so long."

I know he's referring to my ride with Dark Crow. "I'm fine," I assure him, then redirect my attention to my purse. It's a big reservation but a small community. If everything is still here— money, cell phone and all—I'll be amazed. Yet I know, intuitively, that it is. The idea that perhaps there is a path being laid out for me, by the Holy People or just with the help of mere mortals, leaves me both excited and unsettled.

Nelson looks to his jeep. "Wanna ride?"

"Yeah. I'll be right back," I say, then turn toward the ticket counter.

"You don't need no ticket," he suggests at nearly a whisper. He walks to the end of the jeep and offers me a hand up the unfolded metal steps at the back. I feel like Cinderella at the ball, my heavy metal magic coach waiting. I settle into the last seat. From the side of the truck, he speaks again. "This'll get you about two-thirds into where you gotta go. Be on foot from there." He looks at me as if wanting an agreement to the deal.

I nod, taking what I can get. He slaps the metal coach and says, "Here we go folks, hold on to your hats."

Though the jeep is nearly full, I am left with a two-seater to myself. As Nelson drives to the mouth of the canyon, I can't help but look for Dark Crow's truck. His energy is hard to shake. I wonder when the whole thing will hit me.

We drive a quarter mile in, then pull under a tree. Already the sun is blazing. As I take out one of Wyunetta's skirts to create a makeshift head covering, Nelson begins his speech with a well-rehearsed enthusiasm. With tour guide authority, he explains the difference between a petroglyph (etchings marked in the canyon wall) and a pictograph (paintings on the wall), discusses growing crops and storage facilities, and finally speaks of the long walk of 1864, led by the U.S. military.

"More than eight thousand Navajos walked a distance of three hundred miles to a place we call Hweldi," he says in somber tones, as if this part can still get to him, "which means a very hard suffering place. When we were allowed to return to our land and our sacred mountains four years later, my people burst into tears and offered prayers. It was a time of great joy."

He allows a moment of silence to reflect on the suffering and the joy of homecoming. Then, shifting his hat, he returns to his task. "Okay, folks, on we go."

We pull out again, making further inroads on the well-trod sandy canyon floor. The walls grow higher and higher. I, like the rest of the tourists, begin to get into it, forgetting where I've come from and where I'm going. We turn another curve, and I let go a little more, allowing the awe of the canyon to run over me, mark me like the Desert Varnish that streams down the upper edges of the canyon walls. Nelson yells back to us that though they look like wet streaks from rain, they are actually formed by manganese. He says his grandmother called it Mother Earth's hair.

That does it. I'm gone, enchanted with Mother Earth's hair, and all her handiwork, finally and fully seduced. I imagine Nelson's grandmother, who he says grew up here, as a strong, stout woman. I like that the Navajo women are equal to the men, owning and passing down the land through the matriarchs. They are greatly admired and appreciated for weaving the rugs that, in the current economy, are often the bread and butter for a whole family. But best of all, they tell some of the finest stories I've heard.

It seems like only yesterday I was at the Smithsonian watching a small group of women elders weaving their rugs, telling stories of creation and the Navajo way of life. It was in large part what prompted me to consider a career that involved studying indigenous peoples. Both the storytelling and the rug weaving had a rhythm, created with a calm assurance that there is an order to things. I came away with the feeling that if I could just get into the flow of life and pay attention to this order, everything would work itself out. The feeling resurrects in me now, in this vast cut-out of red and gold earth, pointing me toward hope.

There is so much here, so much to believe in, even if it's only the awe of the moment. I tilt back my head on the seat, wanting to laugh aloud. Enchanting. I breathe intentionally, full and deep, as the canyon walls leap higher and higher, engulfing us in a living, breathing theatre of nature.

Only my companions distract me with their video cameras and big floppy hats. A whiff of coconut oil hits my nostrils, offending my senses. I want to smell the land, not fake botanicals. I wonder what the ancestors must think of all this tourism. People paying forty bucks a pop to truck in and gaze at their land, hear the bare facts of their culture and lives, and then go out, impressed but unchanged, to participate in the competitive materialism that is killing the very land they hope somebody else saves.

I notice my emotions turning sour. The well-oiled young woman in front of me is the source of my irritation. I think of cancer in the years ahead as she squeezes more oil from her oversized bottle. Psychic insight, perhaps, but also plain old logic. It makes me curious, so I take a closer look into her future, allowing my eyes to lose focus, going within.

Yes, there is cancer. Of the throat, though, not skin. And it's a good thirty years ahead. She will be terrified, as will her husband and children, who as yet do not exist in her life. The illness will be her spiritual wake-up call. So late in life. Too bad.

Something inside prompts me, and I remember a mystic once telling me that to see the future is only half the gift. Along side each insight is the power to help change what is not desired. And along with that, the responsibility to discern if that is what you are being called to do. In this case, I feel it is appropriate to send a prayer on her behalf. I set aside my irritation with her and pray she does not have to wait so long to get to know her own soul. I don't pray for a softer call, since that is not up to me, and she may need death itself to break through to her. Death has a way of doing that to you, whether it's your own death or that of someone you love. I ought to know.

The grandeur of our surroundings overtakes me again. God, but there is a polarity in this place. From awe to irritation to prayer to grandeur in under three minutes. Kind of scary, especially when I remember the Grand Canyon's effect on me.

Nelson stops the jeep along the muddy trail. Again he performs his duty as tour guide, spouting out the facts and myths, adding a few jokes. My guess is that he would rather just let us all gape, open-mouthed, watching us appreciate what is undoubtedly sacred to him. But his tips don't come from allowing the sacred to move the average tourist's soul. They come from brazen driving, spouting facts and rehearsed jokes and letting the loud-mouthed jerk who insisted on the front seat call him "boy" instead of Nelson.

Those tips will no doubt feed our tour guide's family. Like the rest of humanity, he does what he has to do. It's taking its toll on him, though. I can see it in the way he shifts his hat so no one can really look into his eyes, and in the way he lights a cigarette and sighs after the first long drag.

"The sacred becomes mundane," I whisper to no one listening, then reply to myself, "Ain't it the truth."

I feel myself becoming negative again, even angry. God, I'm a damn ping-pong ball out here. Maybe it's just that I did not take my death threat with Dark Crow seriously enough and it is catching up to me. Then again, maybe I'm really losing it and just don't know it, because everything is moving too fast. It scares me, like these huge walls of earth scare me when we get too close. What keeps such massive walls from crashing in, anyway?

"We won't be going to Massacre Cave today," Nelson says, "that's up the left arm of the canyon in what is called Canyon Del Muerto, which means canyon of the dead, but people like to hear the story. Most of the men had gone out hunting and left the old men and the women and children on a high ledge. The Spanish troops passed by and a Navajo woman started shouting at them. The Spanish couldn't get up there, so they fired shots into the ledge, killing most of them. More than a hundred Navajos died up there. Today, we believe it is still chindi, what you might call haunted."

"Lovely," I whisper, my mood in another dive. Even more ghosts to contend with, assuming they see the whole canyon as their stomping grounds. Not to mention people who like to hear such stories sitting right in front of me.

We move on and stop again at the next set of ruins, clay brick houses tucked halfway up the canyon in alcoves inaccessible without hand and toe holds. Here the Anasazi cooked and told stories and had babies and hid from enemies. I look up, past the ruins that spook me, craning my neck to see the top of the canyon ridge.

Without warning, the truck tilts, as if quicksand has swallowed its left side. My stomach stays upright, making me nauseous. I look around. Everyone appears tilted to one side, yet no one else seems to notice. My brain feels like a salad being wrung out in a spinner.

Vertigo. The walls lean and loom, like ghosts themselves, threatening. "How dare you?" they seem to scream, animated, alive. My stomach shifts, my heart pumping blood the weight of oil. A light sweat breaks across my shoulders, upper lip and forehead.

Losing my center, an internal dam breaks. Fear rushes in like a flash flood. The Anasazi are watching from their clay mini-villages tucked into those impossible cliffs half way up the walls. I know it. I can feel them. How many? Why are they still here? What do they want from me?

As if on cue, Nelson explains how he got stuck in one of these forbidden places as a child, his knees suddenly too weak to move, sure that the ghosts were out to get him, as his parents had sternly warned. My heart trembles in place, my courage sucked out by the throat.

I place my head between my knees, hearing a tourist ask, "Do you really believe in ghosts?" He responds by bending at the knees, which produces a creak that sounds to me like a gun ricocheting off the canyon walls.

"It's just the vertigo," I say to myself. "Just a normal bodily reaction to the eyes losing correct perception."

A wisp of cloud swoops down at me, racing under my nose. I will myself to breathe deeply and evenly. If the vertigo passes, maybe the ghosts will go, too. I swallow on a dry throat, see my finger shake.

I hear Nelson beside me just as he grabs a shoulder. "Happens to some," he whispers to me, then shoves hard, holding on to one arm so I don't fly off the seat. Like a miracle, an energy moves through his hands from my left shoulder to my center, pushing the vertigo out my right shoulder. I look up at him in awe. A healer?

Without another word, he goes back to his cab, starts the engine, and pulls out. I sit upright and stare, dumbfounded. I feel perfectly fine. Only my soaked shirt offers any evidence of what I've been through. Not that I'm likely to forget it.

After a bathroom break at what is probably the only modern facility out here, constructed just for us tourists, we go again.

Soon enough, there it is. Spider Rock, jutting up out of the canyon center. A towering pillar that must have somehow demanded, as the earth fell away, to stay right where it was. No wonder the Holy People are reported to have taken up residence here.

End of the line for me. But I'm not ready. Fear still has me, even if the vertigo is gone. There are ghosts out there, by God, if only in the form of energy-charged wisps of cloud. More than I want to contend with.

Nelson puts down the stairs and helps everyone off. I wait for the others to go first. When it is my turn, he gives my hand a squeeze. "Tough ride," he says, smiling and squatting to crack his knees. I smile a plastic smile, not finding it funny at all.

"Where do I go from here?" I ask nervously, looking further

in to the canyon, its walls now monstrously high. Still, the vertigo seems far off, as if kept at bay, unable to reach me anymore. I am grateful beyond measure.

"Further east, about a half dozen miles. Just keep going in. Got a kid coming to meet you. There's quicksand with the rain yesterday. Not more than a few feet deep, but it can be troublesome. He knows how to get past it. Got in it enough times himself."

A half dozen miles more? He must be joking. I want to tell him how crazy it is, that I'm not The One, that at least Chief ought to have met me here, even though I can plainly see a truck won't go much beyond where we are now. Ahead, the terrain grows over the path, then it appears there is no path. What the hell have I gotten myself into?

Nelson puts a hand on my shoulder, as if he can see my turmoil and wants to express his sympathy. I'm grateful enough to keep quiet and be on with it. I look at the woman with a wake-up call thirty years down the road and know I can't avoid mine, right here and now. Still, I want to stall, keep that healing hand on me as long as I can. Besides, I have a lot of questions I'd rather have answered before I meet the Chief. Not the least of them being who he is really expecting, since I know I'm not The One.

"So how did this Chief describe me? A tall, dark-haired white woman?"

He looks at me quizzically. "No."

"Then how?"

"Said I'd feel a soul that matched his. I felt that when you shook my hand."

"Oh," I say.

His smile widens, as if knowing he has unnerved me. "Here's some water. Gets hot out there, and unless you get a natural spring, the creek water isn't safe." He hands me a plastic grocery bag with two bottles and points me onward. I wonder how comical I must look, a fair-skinned woman in moccasins with a makeshift headdress hanging on for dear life to a backpack, plastic bag and a grease-stained purse.

Just get on with it.

Right. I thank Nelson for his generosity, look boldly into

the distance, offer up my standard catchall "Amen" and begin walking into the vast beauty that terrifies me. If the shifting sand beneath my feet is a metaphor—or worse, an outright sign—I don't want to know.

From behind me, Nelson calls out a stern "Be on the lookout for mountain lions in there." I listen for a follow-up laugh, like it's a joke. It does not come.

10

The jeep roars off without me. Ahead lie a kid, a Chief and wild animals. "Lions, Chiefs and kids, oh my," I say as though I were Dorothy, then laugh at myself. Truth be told, I am less afraid of the lions out in the wilderness than the biggest lion—the canyon herself. Indeed, it feels as if, walking into this wide opening of earth, I am walking into the mouth of a lion. There seems to be a strange sense of assurance about it, though. Not an assurance that I won't be eaten alive, but that if I am eaten, I will like it. Be glad, even, to have been digested in her belly and shit out, anew. That is how the shamans I have known would put it, anyway.

As I walk, I draw on their many words of prophecy. I, too, am a shaman, they said. Though I have never actually tested their theory, it comforts me. Even if I don't believe in me, I believe in them. At least some of them. At least some of the time. So I'm a part-time believer once-removed. Sounds about right.

I breathe in and out again, a kind of acceptance of this shamanic death-walk, this death and rebirth. Why it will happen in this wind- and water-carved sanctuary of earth, as opposed to the many other sacred places I have visited, I don't know. I just feel it. Here I will die. And if it does not kill me, it will be a good thing.

I take a drink of the already warm water and take in the scent of sagebrush and peaches as I walk, putting one foot in front of the other. Without effort, I seem to fly up and away into my bird-self. I float higher and higher, yet somehow also deeper into the here and now. It might be a dangerous thing to do out here in the wilderness, with how far you can drift from your fight-or-flight instincts. Yet instead of falling into the fear,

I simply witness it down there, in Mary Margaret, and let it go.

Time passes almost without notice. The high, time-lined walls, open blue sky and wild canyon floor create an optical illusion. It seems that I have moved nowhere despite walking and stopping for short swallows of water. The sun seems to be moving, too, but of that I am not even sure. The canyon bends so much, it is hard to tell. And where is the boy that has been promised?

As if on cue, he appears. Five years old or so, sliding out of nowhere, making me jump clean out of my skin. My bird-self slams back into reality. Damn, I've got to learn some re-entry skills one of these days.

The boy giggles to my startled jump, his brown, naked shoulders bouncing as he covers his mouth with his hand.

"Hi there," I stammer. "Where did you come from?"

"I'm pretty sure I was an angel before this lifetime," he says matter-of-factly. I immediately wonder what kind of life he has lived to have ideas of "angels" and "before this lifetime." Seems more New Age than Navajo. I also wonder about the scars on his back, long ones the width of shoe laces.

"Oh," I say, "cool."

He beams, and doing so reminds me of someone I knew a long, long time ago. Someone I loved. Perhaps because of this association, I adore him already.

From this point on, I hear everything I could want to know about a five-year-old's interior world. He is called Puck, for the hockey puck he carries in his pocket, which he found at the rim of the canyon while out exploring one day at the ripe old age of three. He has never seen a hockey game but has heard about them and all that fighting so you hardly have any teeth when you are done, and aren't I very tall and very white, and his father got their truck that never works at a place called "Damn Tuba City," and he knows some people who would sell me very pretty necklaces if I have lots of money, or even a little.

I begin to respond, but there is no time before my little companion has moved on to the intricate instructions for hanging a tire swing from a tree, which his mother did completely wrong, and even his uncle did not get right the first time.

The boy reminds me of Hannah, my best childhood friend. She was an angel, too. Or so I thought back then. Maybe still do. We met when we were both eight, me shy and uncertain of the world, she already full-blast into the adventure of it. She talked a mile a minute with no gaps in conversation long enough for me to interject an idea of my own. Hardly time to have one.

I didn't mind. Hannah saw everything from every angle. To view life through her eyes was a wonder indeed. In fact, I'd go so far as to say she taught me to see, though I never even began to approach her degree of mastery. It was because of her that I began to love crystals. She'd heard that Jesus had claimed that if the people would not praise him, the rocks would cry out. Far more spiritual than I, she decided rocks, especially the pretty ones, must have something to say. The least we could do was listen.

Puck also reminds me of Hannah because of the promise I made to her. Rather, I made a promise to God. But in those days, Hannah and God were much the same to me. She was, so far as I knew, the only person who really loved me. God was reputed to do the same. They merged in my mind, and heart, as a result.

We were twelve by the time of my great promise. Hannah, who attended St. Agnes with me, had decided that we needed to give up something extraordinary for Lent that year. She said we ought to consider our hearts very thoroughly, then give up that which we most treasured. And not only give it up for Lent, but for always, our whole life. She was very serious about it. I became just as serious.

I ought to have known that she'd think of something far better than I ever could. But I had this fantasy that if I tried hard enough, I would be able to outdo her. She would think up something good, all right. It would no doubt be a profound statement about herself, and the world as well. So I had to give up what I held dearest to me—not in an effort to compete, but in an effort to prove my worthiness. Whatever I gave up, it would certainly have to make a statement about the world, but it had to go further. It had to be something that would help change the world, at least a little. Only then would I be able to hope to match my beloved Hannah.

When the day came, I had it. I knew I would be giving up something greater than she could possibly dream of. I would give up having children. I would make my statement about the world by saying it was a crappy place that was already over-populated. I would not bring one more child into it. Even Hannah could not know how much this cost me, for I was certain she did not feel the same tugs at her heart any time we saw a baby in the mall. Or feel, as I did, a symbiotic wonder as a pregnant woman waddled by. Surely Hannah could not outdo the primordial mother within me giving up her unborn.

I was wrong. Hannah, in that twisted way she had of seeing life upside down as right side up, gave up guilt for Lent. "Not the guilt that guides us to do right," she explained, "but the guilt that would make us feel unworthy, and so keep us afraid of attempting anything truly great." I had offered God another baby or two, which the world didn't need anyway. Hannah offered God the human condition. I beamed in pride to know such a great being as she.

When she was raped and murdered on Good Friday by a man they never caught, I vowed to keep my lifelong Lent in her honor. A cold chill runs through me as I remember.

Yet for the first time, it is warmed by this beautiful boy Puck. In his exuberant childhood beingness, he reminds me not only of Hannah, but of what I gave up for her. With his big brown eyes, and innocent little mouth running a mile a minute, I am acutely aware of how great a sacrifice it is to agree to an empty womb. How much it costs to vow to miss the priceless joy of seeing the world though the eyes of a child you have birthed. One might think I am just holding on to the past to keep such a promise, but there really are too many children in the world. Besides, now more than ever, it is not a world anyone can be thrilled about bringing a child into. Even so, I wish it was guilt I had thought to give up.

I come back from my mental wanderings to find Puck still chatting, now about how angels fly through high vibration, not wings, and did I know that angels can help with anything, but first we must ask, and since most people don't really believe in angels, nobody asks, and that is why life is so hard, when it could be almost as easy here as it is in heaven.

Such talk makes me wonder for a fleeting moment if Puck is really Hannah, reincarnated, though my inner Catholic proctor reminds me that I am not sure I believe in reincarnation at all. The idea of it, of her coming back to me this way, sends goose bumps along my arms. I wonder if, as I was once told, goose bumps are signs that we have stumbled upon a great truth and our bodies are electrified in response. I like the idea and want to grab Puck and tell him how beautiful he is, how priceless, how perfect. He would not understand, so I don't.

The half-walking, half-dodging pits of wet sand goes quickly with Puck as guide and companion until abruptly he stops and says he has to go home. He says Chief will find me from here, and that I am very much like Chief, and the angels must be singing to have us together again, and did he bore me to death during our walk? As he asks, I notice his face cloud and wrinkle with worry. It makes me wonder how many times, with such a chatty nature, he has heard about his "boring people to death."

I smile, as warmly and genuinely as I know how. "Not at all, Puck. I think you are wonderful."

He lets out a huge, happy sigh. "I think you are too," he says, as if I might have been worried as well. Perhaps I was.

He turns to leave, then turns back. "Can I have a hug?" he asks.

Again I am amazed at the innocent needs and offerings of children. I want more than a hug. I want to drink him, swallow his innocence, wear it like perfume. But he is someone else's child, must return to someone else's home. A hug will have to do.

"I would love that," I say, lowering myself down on one knee. We embrace, long and hard. He finally pulls away, still too soon for me.

My bundle of amazing exuberance races off, weaving himself around trees and bush, then disappears. I find myself tearful, feeling much the same about him as I felt about Hannah—that I had looked into the face of God, and God had smiled.

I walk on, reveling in my good fortune. I thank the angels for this unexpected help with my longstanding grief, for Puck said we must not forget to offer our gratitude. "The angels do so much," he had said, and I find myself, at least for the moment, a true believer.

The Lion's Mouth, I realize, has already become my little world. The rest of the humanity may be carrying on as usual. Eric may be finding toy trinkets and Wall Street may be seeing a bull or a bear. But I cannot fathom it here. Past the lion's teeth, the fear is gone. Only wonderment remains.

Again, I am on my own, looking for Chief, considering those who have led me thus far. Jimmy, Wyunetta Morningstar, Dark Crow, Nelson and now beautiful Puck. All warm-up acts for the big show, which ought to begin any time.

The high noon sun shines down, making the canyon sparkle and glow. I realize there is an energy here, something even beyond Puck's jubilance, that has ignited something completely new in me. What is this feeling? I find myself smiling as I realize the answer. Though I have never felt I really understood what the word means, I know what I want to call it.

Home.

11

What I just can't shake is the idea that I'm anything like this Chief. A white woman, born and raised a Catholic in D.C.? What might we have in common? "Soul," Nelson had said. What the hell is that these days? If I knew, I wouldn't be out searching for gurus, that's for sure. Of course, it may be like the Taoists say, that you must give up to succeed.

"Okay, okay, I give up," I yell out to the empty canyon. "Just get me there."

The thought makes me laugh at myself, my mood a slightly cocky, happy-go-lucky giddiness. Puck helped. He really did.

I have walked another mile at least since the little package of perpetual gladness left me, drifting through this gigantic sandbox of nature as if it were fairy dust. There is no path, no trail, only further in and further still. The last of the Navajo homesteads are miles behind me, leaving me to navigate sun-cracked earth, desert brush, and the constant threat of wildlife. Besides a few turkeys, the Lion's Mouth has so far spared me any great challenge.

My only enemy is the sun bearing down, hot and pene-trating. Each breeze that passes my face seems a caress, a kiss from Oya, the African goddess whose statue was responsible for getting me here in the first place. It brings me to a state of acute thankfulness. The further I walk, the more I become the wonder I feel.

It is as though I am a woman in love, or so I suppose. I've never been. It makes me ponder, for the billionth time, when love will come to me. Or if it will. Other than Hannah, this has been a loveless life. Not a complaint, really. Just a fact I've long accepted. Nothing to get worked up about, especially when you can't change it. At least that is what I tell myself, every damn day.

Ahead in the distance, out in an open area of sand, I see a copper-colored dog resting on the ground, panting heavily in the sun. How hot is it out here? I squint my eyes as I look up to get my bearings on the sun. Mid-afternoon. Pretty hot.

I consider that a dog in the middle of nowhere is likely wild. It ought to frighten me. Yet fear refuses to swell. As I approach the large but skinny beast, my generosity grows, building until a feeling of all-out love blossoms in me. Love, and more love, for everything alive. A sense of oneness with all things. I want to pet the dog, offer it water, share my giddy bliss.

Gaining ground, my vision comes into focus. I am stunned. This is no dog, but a man, curled into a ball on his side, with an animal skin across his shoulders. A skull rides his head like a crown.

"Holy shit, a skinwalker," I whisper to myself. An honest-to-God skinwalker. If I were a Navajo, I'd be frightened out of my mind. Instead, I am intrigued. For the man, I swear, glows.

He is not panting after all, I see, but vomiting in dry heaves.

I am prepared for anything, or so I assume, until a sudden flash of light comes at me, a ripple of white purity emanating from him, like a huge wave on this sea of sand, brilliant and powerful.

> *Time slows. Stops. I see with the eyes of a dreamer. Understand with perfect wisdom. I have gone into myself, as before. I will not remember, I know. Yet it will sustain me, as it has before.*
>
> *The circle of glossy white light approaches in slow motion, a band of pure energy that emanates from him, brighter than bright. Unearthly. Divine. This is what you wait a forever for. Some never feel it. Unity. Oneness. Wholeness. A taste of eternity.*
>
> *Oh, Norbu. Where have you been? So long in coming again. Too long a wait, this time. Too long you have kept yourself from me. Too long. Didn't you know my need? Feel my thirst? Test these cracking bones to*

see how long they have been without your marrow.
Oh, Norbu! Oh, Love! To know you again—this alone
is my sustenance, this alone the reason I survive.

We are one and the same, are we not? Yet where is
our third? Norbu, Norbu, still incomplete. My heart
cries for longing, even as it fills with you. There is
more to us, Norbu. Where have we gone?

A shudder of delight hits me, an assault of love.
Pure orgasm exploding in every cell of my being,
bursting forth. The wave cuts through me at the base
of my spine, my hips and stomach, and through my
heart, throat and forehead, all at once. The feeling rips
through me in a split second and is gone.

I shudder with my whole body. Something has happened. What, I don't know. But something. Something profound, beyond profound. Something I want to touch, but can't. Something eternal.

Only once do I recall having felt this before. In Tibet, as I repeatedly prostrated myself before a sixty-foot Buddha. Next to me appeared an aged monk who knelt, bowed, prostrated and returned to standing in perfect time to my motions. It went on from early morning until almost nightfall. We parted without speaking.

It was hot that day, too.

At my hurried pace I am almost upon the man. He is rail thin, ribs showing, with wrinkled skin to prove eighty years of living, at least. He is dressed in loosely fitting natural cotton pants that seem remarkably clean for this place.

Forget the Chief. This is the man I am looking for. I am sure of it. Despite his heaving convulsions, a pure, undiluted love radiates from him, like a glow of energy. No wonder I have been walking in greater and greater bliss. He has been ever closer. Who cares if I am chosen? I am chosen enough to be here, now.

"Who are you?" I ask, though I ought to be offering assistance.

"Chief," he says between heavy breaths, then looks at me. "Who are you?"

I am breathing heavily, too, yet this stops me short, Chief? But he's a white man. Well-tanned from the sun, but certainly not a Navajo. And he wants to know who I am? If this is Chief, didn't he send for me? Didn't he tell Jimmy and all the others I was to come find him? Would he not know me?

Ah, but of course. He can see, now that I am here, I am not The One. The sinking feeling comes back, settles in my gut.

Chief grins like a child as if to say "Got you," then retches again.

When he returns his gaze to my face, it has an apology in it. "Skinwalker's speed," he offers as explanation. "I am not as good as I once was."

I gape. He admits to being a skinwalker? Just like that? "You have to be careful," I warn, like I know anything, "admitting to skinwalking in these parts." I ought to be wary of him. But who can be wary of a man who emanates light like a forty-watt soft glow in all directions?

"Old school skinwalker," he says. "When it was taught to me, it was not abused as it is now."

"Oh" I say, remembering having heard something like that. In the old days, skinwalkers were the good guys. They took on the skins of the animals they wanted power from in order to travel to places faster than a human could. I suppose this guy is old enough to be old school.

"Can I help you?" I finally ask.

"Give me a minute," he says, one hand patting the air, as if to wave off my offer.

Yet I feel compelled to do something. Anything. So I squat near him, my knees an inch from his holy heaving frame, and spread my hands above his body. I've no idea why I am doing this, only that I was once told by a proof-positive Mayan healer from Guatemala that I have healing abilities, too. My hands could work miracles if I would only use them, she said, a little miffed I hadn't figured this out already. I'm not so certain as she was, but this man deserves anything I have any chance of providing. At minimum, I can reflect his own beauty back to him, thus helping him heal himself.

I watch his body grow calm, his breathing more even. He looks into my eyes with a love that could melt the whole world's hard heart. Why is it the true Masters hide away?

"Thank you," he says to me in a gently aged voice. With a shaky hand to my cheek, he adds: "Beautiful."

I take a quick shot of breath into my lungs and promptly tears spring forth. Me, who cries maybe once a season, moved to tears so easily this day. In his remark, the Lion's Mouth closes, swallowing me whole. I bask in a sense of belonging I cannot explain.

"Who are you?" I ask again, almost whispering, wanting something more than name and occupation, or whatever "Chief" is meant to imply.

I try to look at his face to determine something more of who he is, but I can't. His eyes are like magnets. Crystal blue, lake deep and somehow familiar. Like I've seen them before. When my gaze gets even close to his face, they jump to the eyes and cannot disengage.

"Who are you?" he returns again, all the more serious.

This time I get it. He's not asking who I am, as in Mary Margaret Hathaway, but who I am as in *who I am*. For that, I have no answer, no idea. A thousand years with him and maybe I'll know.

"I'm Mary. Are you okay?"

He sits up slowly, testing to see if his bony arms will hold him up. They do.

"Sweet Mary. I have waited so long."

In an instant, my heart falls. I will, after all, have to tell him that I am not The One he thinks. How I wish I was, now more than ever.

He laughs, more heartily than one might expect of a man in his eighties.

"You are The One, and I am well beyond eighty. I am one hundred and eight years old," he says.

"Wow," I say, not knowing what else to say. The idea that he reads my mind is spooky, though it does not surprise me. Great men need no words to understand the hearts and minds of lesser beings. Even white men, though I am a bit disappointed in that. Maybe his features and darker skin tone have just faded with the years. Yet why should I care?

"I am not indigenous and I am not *not* indigenous. I am

Chief Of No Tribe," he says, adding somewhat sternly, "and you are no lesser being."

Will this be a one-way conversation, I wonder? Me thinking, he answering.

"It will be however you dream it. Your choice, always."

"This is too bizarre," I say, not so much to him but to the air. Actually, I kind of like the mind reading, what with words being such a limited form of communication.

He smiles, blue eyes flashing a wallop of love, energy and serenity in equal portions. Magic. Pure, glowing magic.

Wait! Magic blue eyes. Isn't that what Eric had said of my own, only yesterday? It takes me about two seconds to realize whose eyes Chief's remind me of. My own. I swear to God, I'm looking into my own eyes. There is more behind his, much more. More soul. More peace. More intelligence. More consciousness. But the actual eyeballs, given a few years difference in wear and tear, are the same. It gives me a weird feeling. Like somehow, we do match.

He sits tall now, without the aid of his arms, as thin as Gandhi on a fast. Again he seems old, yet he feels ageless. As usual, I find myself wanting to understand, when I know I'd do better to just give up. I'm way out of my league. Way, way out.

"This is all the bi-locating I can take, Sweet Mary. You'll see me again, a few more miles in at my homestead. I'll be waiting."

He hardly looks well enough to stand, let alone walk. And what is this "bi-locating?" I remember learning something back in grade school about Saint Francis of Assisi doing that. Is this guy a saint?

"I will be fine," he says to my unspoken concern, pulling the animal skin around his shoulders tighter. "I have four legs to carry me. Besides, I'm still back there, too, so it's really just a matter of letting this 'me' go."

I laugh. This is impossible. Yet I am, for whatever reason, willing to put the absurdity aside for a moment.

"Why did you come, if it made you so sick?"

"Love paves the way," he answers gently, "however alone we believe ourselves to be."

With that, he rolls over onto all fours, melds into the dog skin until he is, by God, a dog, and trots off. A few seconds more and he has vanished.

"No way," I say aloud, shaking my head to no one. "No way in hell."

12

"Know what you know," I hear on the wind in Chief's wonderful voice.

"As if I know what that means!" I respond, laughing, shaking my head, trying to comprehend the impossible.

I look around in every direction, yet see only empty canyon. The wind blows gently, birds ride the thermal air patterns and caw, the sun continues to move through the day, all as if life is normal. Like I didn't just see a bi-locating skinwalker with my own magic blue eyes. Like I wasn't just witness to a Holy Mother Of God miracle that occurred right in front of me.

He was here. Wasn't he?

I stare up at the hot sun, forgetting to shield my eyes, then away again quickly, my retinas burning.

Impossible. Yet it happened. Didn't it?

I lift my water bottle to my lips. It's empty. Reaching for the second one, I find it empty, too. When did that happen?

A fear begins to turn my stomach and then rises, grabbing me by my parched throat. Am I suffering from heat exhaustion without realizing it? They say being alone in such temperatures can bring about all kinds of strange imaginations, especially in places like these, where spirits haunt the sacred earth.

Did I see a ghost?

I swallow, expecting to feel thirsty, but I don't. Why don't I? Why do I feel fine? Good, even? I direct my attention to the rest of my body, searching for signs of heat stroke or exhaustion. I feel none. Just a tingling sensation surrounding me, a light energy extending a few feet from me in every direction.

Like I'm the one who glows.

"No way," I hear myself say several times more, speaking to

the vast emptiness that surrounds me.

Know what you know, the wind-turned-Chief, or Chief-turned-wind, had said. For whatever reason, for reasons beyond reason, my heart feels certain of its course. Joy surges, palpable, as if a strong electrical current is pushing my pulse along a happy, winding river. My smile widens, stupid and innocent. Without warning, my feet move beneath me, taking me deeper into the canyon.

So, this is what it feels like to pull the last dark card of Shoot The Moon, eh? Maybe it is the card of insanity, but I never dreamed the jackpot could be so wild. My only fear is, coming down from this high, learning that none of it is real. How could anyone face "reality" after conversing with one such as he?

I bask in the thought until a shrill sound seems to further split the canyon apart. I can't imagine where it is coming from, until I realize it is the cell phone Eric gave me. I fumble through my purse for it, knowing I am facing another miracle. The phone, if turned on at all, surely would have lost its battery by now. Besides, there is no way I'm going to get a connection in the depth of this canyon.

If it's Chief, I'm going to know I'm in the middle of "Oh, God, Part V" and promptly turn around to check myself into a mental institution.

It is not Chief. It's Eric.

"How are you?" he asks, sounding pleasant and normal, a man who lives in a world where shapeshifting bi-locaters are still in the realm of the impossible. "Find what you were look-ing for?"

"I guess," I say, hearing myself sounding a little shell-shocked. I had thought I would sound a little better, more upbeat, given that's how I feel. The discrepancy alarms me.

"Are you okay, Mary? You don't sound good."

"Don't I?" I reply weakly. Eric and Chief simply don't compute. Suddenly I'm confused, unsure of anything, aware of how bizarre the truth I've just experienced would sound to Eric. They would cart me away. Perhaps they should.

"It's hot," I say.

"Where are you Mary? I'm coming to get you." There is

insistence in his voice, but it does not reach me.

"Canyon de Chelly. Dark Crow brought me. But I'm all right."

"You don't sound all right, Mary. In fact, you don't sound good at all." It is Eric that seems not all right to me now. I've no energy for that.

"Yeah, okay," I say, "I'll call you." I find the end button, then the power. I check again, to make sure it is off. It is. Maybe always was. Maybe I dreamed it all. Maybe.

Truth is, I could be dreaming, still in the back of Dark Crow's cold flatbed on a lonesome side road. That would make more sense than this.

Well, at least I see the situation for what it is. I'm in quicksand of a kind I can't even fathom. Yet it is all I've wanted, what I have searched a decade—no, a lifetime—to find. If I'm going to go down, let it be with the likes of Chief Of No Tribe. He's my people. I understand that now. Maybe, if the gods are kind at all, and even though I'm not The One, I'm his. The thought takes me into the bird. I fly aloft, as Mary Margaret puts one foot in front of the other, down there. The miles pass in an instant when you are flying.

The instant over, I find myself approaching Chief's makeshift homestead. At least I hope it is his. I glance around the lean-to made of logs and brush. Not much, but it offers shade at the edge of an open area. Under it, two bedrolls are laid out, simple but inviting. I'm tired, too. Really.

A small tree stump, turned into a coffee table, sports a well-singed coffee pot, a bucket of water and two cups. Several feet in front of this "living room" there is a dug-out hole, a fireplace circled in stones. Ashes blow in the slight breeze.

My eyes are drawn, if not fully seduced, by the water, but my mind is working in high gear. The answer to my question of insanity seems easy enough. Either the Chief I meet here will be the man I saw back there, or he won't.

If he is, I've found my teacher, my Master, at last. If he isn't, I need to get some water very quickly, then ask for assistance out of the canyon and into a hospital. If they extend the white coat and lace my arms around my body for my own protection, so be it.

I've heard of this before, the spiritual madness that precedes enlightenment. They say all the Great Ones have to go through it. I'm no Great One, but I might as well think of it as an honor to be walking such a similar narrow precipice. Insanity for the sake of enlightenment. The words of the Sufi poet Rumi swirl inside my brain like a fine wine beneath the nose. "This fire I crackle in is You. I burn as You, burning away myself...Mad lucidities! Triumphs without sound! Don't look for me; I am not here."

"Welcome," comes a voice from beyond the trees, breaking my spell and cracking open my heart in the same instant.

Tears would pour if there were any water left in me. Chief moves from the trees to stand before me, a man in the flesh. Smiling and extending his arms, he looks like a grandfather expecting his favorite daughter's daughter. He is still alarmingly thin, but his golden tan set against his clean cotton pants and a flowing shirt gives him the appearance of perfectly sound health. That, and the glow.

I can't move, only stand and stare. I know I need water, and before the end, may also need the asylum. For now, though, I have arrived at my beginning. I shiver as goose bumps cover my body.

Yet with them, another sensation comes. Something I don't like. Something inside, growing dark. Like a seed in my heart, an ugly thing that expands. Suddenly, ignited like a brush fire, it moves quickly down into my gut, up into my brain, taking me over. I step back, giving voice to a rapidly consuming vehemence.

"Who the hell are you?"

13

The urgent brush fire of bitterness is eating me alive, threatening to attack the very Master I have sought. I wonder if he can take it, the hate that he brings up, and half don't give a damn if he can or can't. He's hidden himself too long, and the starving wolf I have become is poised for a verbal killing spree.

"You need water," Chief replies to my venom, smiling, filling one of the small tin cups with water and extending it toward me. I have half a mind to send it careening from him with a wild swoop of my hand.

"Are you a bodhisattva?" I demand, both wanting and hating the cup in his hand.

His forehead wrinkles, as if in uncertainty. "A bodhisattva? Who do you say that I am?"

"Oh, lovely!" I sneer, throwing my hands up in the air, turning toward the canyon wall behind me, as if it is an entity in and of itself, one that will understand. "He borrows the words of Christ and doesn't even know what a damn bodhisattva is!"

I turn back to him, vengeance oozing out of me, hands on my hips, demanding answers to questions I have not even asked.

Chief looks mildly amused, like a loving parent might look upon the tantrum of a child. This pisses me off even further, as does the humor in his voice when he speaks.

"Bodhisattva," he says, as though in a spelling bee. "A being of enlightenment destined to become a Buddha who has forgone the bliss of Nirvana in order to save all children of God on earth."

His academic answer infuriates me. "Well, are you?" I scream, totally out of control.

"I wouldn't call it that," he says, again pointing to the cup. "Have some water, please, Sweet Mary."

The "Sweet Mary" tugs at my heart as a violin pulls pain from a grieving widow. Yet this emotional ploy makes me livid. I want to lunge at him, rip him apart to find the diamonds I suspect inside.

"Yes, that is more like it," he says.

"Don't read my mind!" I scream again, with the ferocious anger you can only feel toward someone you love with passionate devotion. Someone you believe has betrayed you.

He nods his agreement.

"Oh, great, a goddamned mind-reading, 'wouldn't really call it that' bodhisattva who wants to patronize the hell out of me!" My arms flail to punctuate my words, making me feel all the more out of control.

At the "goddamned," his smile disappears into a sad expression. He raises his hand above his head and mine. In a slow movement his arms begin to dance, fluid and strong, in front of me. He appears to wipe away something between us, from our heads down to our feet. As his hand moves, calm enters me from the crown, draining down, the anger moving out through my feet as he pats the ground to each side, then at the back and front of them.

He nods. "Yes, yes, give it to The Mother. The Mother knows what to do with it."

I whimper at the thought, at Mother Earth knowing what to do with my pain and fury, when I have no idea. In seconds I am limp, spent, broken and healed all at once. Tears come despite my parched state. Old, old tears. Old, old sadness.

"Why did you make me wait so long?" I ask him, hearing myself sound pathetic.

Chief extends the cup yet again. This time I reach for it. The tin, cool from the wetness within, is pure delight to my lips and tongue. Suddenly, I am wildly thirsty, gulping breathless, as unselfconscious as a beggar.

"Not too fast," he says tenderly, pointing to a log so I may sit.

I do, fully ashamed to have spoken as I have.

He shakes his head. "It's all right. There is a bond between us that you are not accustomed to. It unsettles old emotions. Stirs them up like a big, messy soup. They have to go somewhere."

I smile, liking the idea.

He smiles in return. "It is good to see you again."

I wonder at the refreshment I feel, suspecting it goes beyond what the water has offered. It is Chief that cools in this terrible desert heat, and no doubt warms when winter sends a chill. It makes me want to curl up and sleep, protected from all that could harm me, even myself.

"There is much to learn," he says, as if beginning to explain a great secret, "and many journeys to make."

"Mmm," I say, forgetting even what we are talking about, feeling an easy but sleepy acceptance. The birds lull me with their song. Has he put something in my drink? No, no, it is him. Only him. Beloved Chief. A Master of Masters.

"Sweet Mary, you are all the Master I am."

I ought to bristle at this, reject the idea out of hand. If he knew my life, all that I have done, and not done, he would not say such things. Instead, I don't respond at all. My eyes drop closed. I force them open wide, trying not to blink. In truth, I want nothing more than to rest here, now, under the watch of this great soul.

I again notice the bed rolls in the shade and move to lie on one. The earth below the slim mat feels like velvet beneath me, the air like silk moving into and out of my lungs. Every hell I've known has been worth this moment. Somehow, all along, I've known it was coming. Only feared I could not wait.

"Yes, sleep," my new, great friend says, following me to the shade.

"I'm sorry I'm so tired. It's only afternoon, isn't it?"

"Shhh...." Chief says, like a caress.

So I shush. Soon, I sleep.

Who knows how long I sleep on and off? Between naps, I cannot pull fully awake, yet I want to ask questions of every sort. Why now? Why here, on the reservation? What does God want from us? Is there a plan? Can we know God? What have I come to do in this life?

I am cared for with ever-full cups of water and gentle

murmurings throughout the day and into the night. Sometime late, I wake to see Chief tend the fire. In the yellow-red light, his glow becomes one with it. I struggle to wake, wanting to speak to him about anything and everything. My life growing up. How long I have waited for some kind of comfort. How much it means to me, now that he is here.

"I know," he says, patting me gently, and "Shhh," and "Later."

Finally, I feel myself drift to a deeper sleep, content and sure that, though I am not the one he seeks, he is the one I have sought after, always.

14

I awake to a blanket of stars, a steady fire and Chief moving about me. The night wind keeps the fire crackling. My shoulders chilled, I pull the blanket from beneath me and watch him. If there is any sickness left in him, there is no evidence of it. He moves with ease, even grace, and yet carefully, as if each step is sacred. I once saw a Tai Chi Master I knew in a grocery store and watched how he moved, selecting vegetables with more care than I could have imagined feeling for another human being, let alone a vegetable. I was impressed but could not relate it to my own experience. Food to me is a utility, even when it tastes great.

"Your mistake," Chief says, breaking my thought gently, "is not a matter of your depth of care. It is in viewing a vegetable as less valuable than a human being. It is the mistake of humanity. It may cost us the world."

He moves as he speaks, collecting sticks, bowing ever so slightly as he offers each one to the fire. "Everything is sacred," he continues, his voice as gentle and clear as the night around us. "That is not an ideology. You could not be here without the earth to walk on. You could not be here without the air to breathe. In fact, you are ninety-nine point nine percent air. Our scientists have proven this, using the god of rational reasoning."

He chuckles to himself at this thought, as if rational reasoning were child's play. "After that, you are mostly water, so you could not be here without water. This fire is also needed, for such things as warmth on cold nights and to keep predators away. Yet this is not all. Without the fire inside you, you could not live at ninety-eight point six degrees. When we grow cold, our spirit must leave the body. So fire is not a gift to us, it is us."

I am blown away by his explanation, not to mention his continued telepathy. I like the sound of his words, too, the way they flow from his mouth like water moves along a river, and how carefully he seems to form each one. Another might simply state the words. He calls each one forth with tenderness. I cannot imagine anyone thinking I am like this man. Me, with my "hells" and "damns" and worse, thrown out willy-nilly.

I sigh, preferring to contemplate him than ever think of myself again. I cannot trace an accent. Did he grow up moving from country to country, starting as a small boy, maybe? The idea matches my image of him, for there seems a trace of everywhere in him, and no dominance of any region or dialect. But then, he speaks with such calm authority it is hard to get past how it makes you feel long enough to analyze it. Like trying to look at his face, and seeing only eyes. All I know for sure is that I could listen a lifetime, grateful to carry water and chop wood for the privilege.

"Do you understand what I am saying?" Chief stops his work to punctuate the question.

My reply is careful, yet the care is born of intent, not fear of getting it wrong. This man evokes no fear. "I have understood the elements and our need to honor them. But I have to say, I have not loved them like you seem to."

"That is because you do not love you. When you love you—all of you, darkness and light—you will love them. They are you. They are me. We are one."

"It is an important message," I say, not wanting to think about not loving myself.

"It is not a message," he says, squatting next to the fire. "It is."

"There are many perspectives in this world," I respond, though it makes me feel shallow.

"Of course," he says with a gentleman's generosity and goes off, gathering more sticks.

I can't help but take it as a personal rejection. I am not as far along as he would like me to be. But then, I am not The One he seeks. She would be farther along than I am. She would love herself, and so the elements. She would get it in a way that, clearly, I don't.

Chief returns holding a large log carefully, as a mother carries her newborn. Offering it to the fire, it is quickly overtaken, causing every sort of snapping and popping. Chief moves to sit across from me, his legs crossed and his hands gently resting on his knees, looking every bit the wise Master.

"What have you learned, Sweet Mary?"

The question startles me. I can say what my degrees are in, give him information about my history, where I am from, who my family was. Any of that. But what have I learned? How do you answer a question like that?

"It would take days for me to cover it all," I say, fudging.

He smiles serenely, as if he's got all the time in the world.

"Well, let's see. I'm a social scientist and I've traveled quite a bit." I don't like how I sound, like I am trying to impress him. "I don't know. I'm just a regular woman, you know, making her way. Trying to learn. Not much to show for it."

Chief nods, seeing my struggle.

"What about you?" I ask.

"What do you wish to know?"

Like a million things. Like the meaning of life. Like if there is a God. I'll save that one for a while, work my way up.

"Are you a Navajo?" I ask.

"No."

"I didn't think so. Then what?"

He shrugs. "A mutt. A little here and there. I did not want to create any bias for myself. No one can claim me. No one can reject me. I am."

"You *decided* your nationality?" I ask, not trying to hide my skepticism.

"As we all do."

"Very New Age," I say.

"New Age?"

"Yeah. That we choose our parents, our life circumstances, our level of intelligence and other abilities, all before we incarnate each time. I've got a problem with that, given my history."

"Know what you know," he says with little intonation.

Again that "know what you know" stuff. I do know what I

know, but there is a lot I don't know. If he knew what he knew, he'd know I was not The One. Which I am sure he does know. But for whatever reason, I have not been booted out of here, and I'm not going until I've been asked to leave. Who's going to pass up lessons with a Master who glows?

"Well," I say, "if that is true, I mean that we choose it all, then I know that I know I am a certified, card-carrying masochist. If you knew my life story...."

Chief gets a flicker in his eye, as though he has hit an intended mark. "It is only a story," he says, "though I would like to see it through your eyes."

Okay, then. How I see it.

"Uh, let's see," I begin, already feeling the drama swirl in my brain. I don't talk much about my history, mostly because I don't find it worth much conversation.

I sigh and begin again. "The woman—or rather child, since she was only fourteen at the time—who gave birth to me would not acknowledge me as her daughter, even when we were both fully grown. No one talked about the circumstances, but you could pick things up at the family reunions if you were listening, which I always was. I only had to see the whole family once a year, but it was required attendance, given I was raised by my mother's uncle and everyone wanted to make sure he was doing a good enough job. He was a lifelong bachelor, a closet homosexual. Very uptight man. Died a few years back."

Chief offers no response beyond a nod, so I go on.

"He was the only one willing to take me, and he lived far enough away from the rest of the family for me not to be a constant reminder of their shame. He agreed to make sure I was raised a good Catholic." I hear my voice softening, waning, as if the thoughts themselves were weakening me. "Like that would redeem the situation somehow."

I sigh again, and do what I always do—look at the bright side, however dim. "He was a good man at heart, but very afraid to love a girl child too much, afraid of how it would look. Even more afraid people would figure out I was the door to his closet. Anyway, he provided for all my needs and kept a tight ship. I stayed out of his way as much as I could."

I look at Chief, who shows no discernible reaction. Like the shrink I was carted off to, after Hannah was killed. It starts something rumbling inside me, the sprouting of that dark seed of anger I experienced before his magic wave of hand.

Put a lid on it.

I swallow and smile nervously.

"A lack of love in childhood," Chief says, "is often a good way to begin a quest for genuine love." He says this as though it is only a possibility. Yet I know he thinks he is right. Like he has any idea. I was the one who endured it, thank you very much. Where was he?

"To choose a fearful homosexual father can assist a soul in learning about confusing gender issues and hiding the true self."

I think on these new ideas for a second, then feel it is too much to assimilate at the moment, and so continue. "George, that's what I called my father, sent me to Catholic school, but the nuns and I didn't exactly see eye-to-eye on much. On anything, really."

Chief nods. "To choose parents who will force a religious paradigm upon a soul often helps the soul reject and then release dogma, ultimately finding the true spiritual self and one's innate compassion."

Resentment bubbles in my gut and my throat. Doesn't he see how hard my life has been? Doesn't he care? Where is *his* compassion?

"Yeah, maybe," I say, a little flippantly, ready to add the crowning tragedy. Surely sympathy will come from this. "Then after my best friend was murdered, I went a little crazy."

"Good," Chief says, seeming genuinely pleased.

"Good?" I repeat. "It was hell. My best friend, gone through who knows what evil acts, leaving me to see things, like spirits flying, darting across my bedroom walls, making me and everyone else think I was nuts."

"Yes, yes, good."

"Why good?" I demand, tossing tiny sticks into the fire with a vengeance, wishing they were explosives. Like the powder keg I am. I remember this same anger from yesterday, as well as my regret at the vehemence when it was spent. But

I don't care. The beast is unleashed. He can wave it away if he so desires.

Chief speaks without emotion. "Losing your tribe, which for you was your friend, is essential to the spiritual path. The grief opens you, like this canyon. Year after year of wearing away, then a happening to split your heart. Seeing the spirits fly is often part of it. Most believe it is their imagination, and therefore unreal. Those who can see them as real are making great progress. For them, this opening is a success. It proves that reality is so much bigger than one is led to believe. One understands, fundamentally, from one's own experience, that the little lens one has been looking through is little indeed. So good, Sweet Mary. How brave of you to choose it."

Indignation rises within me. I rise to match it, pacing. How careless he is being! Doesn't he know the damage my unleashed anger can do? My voice cracks and wavers in reply, yet each word stands as a world unto itself.

"Maybe I did choose my father, and my mother," I say, fighting for logic to stay in its seat. "Masochistic as it was, maybe I did. I'll allow that as a possibility. But I did *not*, in any way, choose to lose my best friend. She was all I had. Everything, in one little body. I would never have chosen for her to die. Never. I loved her."

"Yes," Chief replies, pushing me, reminding me of how I pushed Dark Crow into his Nothin'. "You loved her, of course. You also chose a friend you knew would die young."

"I most certainly did not!" My eyes fill, my lungs constrict. I don't want to talk about this anymore.

"The soul you are talking about, the one you called Hannah in this lifetime...."

How does he know that? How does he know her name? Is he a sorcerer, a black magician? Has he been following me, checking into my background? He's a skinwalker, after all. So what if he glows?

"She is one you have known in many, many lifetimes. She was aware it would be a short life. It was understood you would be needing a great opening in your twelfth year, so she became that catalyst. It was all agreed upon with the greatest of love."

"You're crazy," I say, pounding the earth with Wyunetta's moccasins. "I mean, it's one thing to think of reincarnation in a far-off, it-could-happen kind of way, and maybe you knew a person in more than one life. It is quite another to think all that suffering was actually planned, like love setting you up to fall apart." I toss a huge stick into the fire, hard enough to send the embers flying. "In fact, that is more than crazy. That is sick."

He seems unimpressed with my arguments. "You have fulfilled your contract well," he says matter-of-factly. "Now it can continue."

Despite his age, I have a deep yearning to take a swing at him. I swallow it.

He raises his eyebrows, waiting. I stop pacing to stare, my legs firmly planted on the ground and my arms crossed tight around my chest, holding me in.

"How's that?" I finally demand.

"Wasn't it good to see that bright soul again?"

My knees weaken and bend involuntarily, my stomach caving in as sure as if I'd been slammed with a baseball bat. I know exactly what he means. Puck. His beautiful brown skin, the hug I'd reveled in. I feel myself infused with grief, searing away at me, and yet joy, too. Unable to stand, I squat, gripping the ground to steady myself. I sway to the beat of my heart, the intensity pushing and pulling me. I don't know what to do, what to think. But, God help me, I know what I hope.

"Was it really her?" I finally ask, my voice twelve years old again, fingers shaking, tears welling.

Chief's voice is calm, smooth, almost void of its aged texture. "Was there really any doubt?"

"Yes!" I scream, standing to the naked night, like a wolf howls grief to the moon. "Shit yes. There's always doubt. Doubt makes it all manageable. Doubt keeps the world rational. It keeps you...." I pace again, unable to sit with this idea. "I can't think of what it keeps you, but I know I need it. It saves your ass over and over again."

"It keeps you safe?" Chief asks in a noncommittal tone.

"Yes, hell yes, it keeps you safe. It keeps you from going off the deep end of fantasy. It keeps you from doing stupid things, and getting too full of yourself, and having hope when despair is the only rational response, and...."

"Mary?" Chief interrupts.

"What!?" I snap, looking him in the eyes, searching for something, anything, to hold on to.

"Is it true?"

"How the hell do I know? Why don't you wave that damn hand of yours to get me out of this pain?"

"Because the answer is *in* your pain. Know what you know."

I can't think. Can't see what is real anymore.

"Is it true?" he probes gently. "Is Puck's soul also the soul that was Hannah's?"

"I don't know!" I scream.

Chief stands, looking ten feet tall, steady as a rock. "Yes you do."

I whimper, looking around, frantic, biting my fingernails, wanting out, to never feel like this again, like it felt that day, when they told me. The words fly through my mind, like the ghosts that came after.

Murdered. Struggle. Floating. Naked. Dead.

"Stop this!" I beg. He can do it, I know he can. With one wave of a hand.

"Only in the darkness of what is buried can you find the truth."

"I don't know what to think," I say, feeling like a junkie in need of a fix.

"Of course not," he replies in complete calm. "It is not about thinking. What does your stomach tell you? Is it true?"

My head says it isn't. My heart hopes it is. But my stomach? I put my hands on my center. It feels like a blender on full speed.

"Go beyond the turmoil, to the center."

Desperate, I search for my center, going beyond what is frantic. I find it, clear and sure.

Deep within, I know what I know, as sure as I have known anything.

"Holy Mother of God," I say, not in vain, but gratitude as I automatically calm, even without Chief's wave of hand. "It's true."

15

I awake to early morning light. This time my sleep was clean and dreamless, save the dangling Oya appearing plain as day in front of my third eye three times. Sitting up, I feel clearer than I have in years. I am delighted by the events and ideas that have unfolded, like a welcome mat and a magic carpet rolled into one.

A smile overcomes me as I stretch, remembering the grandest idea, that of Hannah-turned-Puck. It's amazing, to think she...he...whatever...is somewhere out here, breathing the same Arizona air, sleeping under the same sky. I still have some doubt about the reincarnation thing, in my mind. I am trying not to think about it too much, though, paying attention instead to how it feels in my gut.

It feels good. Really, really good. To think, by some amazing grace, I've been blessed to have experienced my beloved friend's vivacious exuberance once again. The idea that she had long ago escaped the horror I have been trapped in since hearing the news of her death creates goose bumps. Another truth. And so what if I'm wrong? If it's just wishful thinking? There is too much delight in even considering it possible.

"You dreamed of Oya," Chief says, fiddling with sticks near the still burning fire. I look at his bedroll, which appears untouched. Is there no such thing as rest for him?

"Yes," I reply, my voice still low from sleep, only now remembering how poorly I treated this great man again. I push my regret aside, for he seems not to hold it against me. "I ordered a statue of her several years before it finally arrived. I'd given up hope on it, actually. Then when it came wrapped in a newspaper that advertised a job on the reservation, I just had a feeling it would lead to something." I grin at him. "It did."

Chief nods. "It was a good sign, her coming to you last

night."

"A sign?" I ask, standing and reaching for the sky, then touching my toes. Still flexible, after all these years.

"She is the goddess of change that you need. You invoked her when you placed your order. For some, most of the masses, such an order would have been a compliment to Oya. Nothing more. You? At your soul's strength? It was an invitation!"

"I don't know about my soul's strength or any invitation. I just thought she looked cool."

He shakes his head. "Sweet Mary. You have no idea what this did for you. This, too, you planned before this lifetime. You and Oya discussed it. An agreement, like the one with Hannah. You did not have a mere passing fancy for a carving. It was the whole reason you were in Africa. You had an appointment with destiny."

"What exactly do you think I invoked?"

He looks to the sky and lifts a hand in reverence. "Oya is the goddess of weather, especially strong weather. Tornadoes! Lightning! Destructive rainstorms! Fire!"

"I know that part."

His eyes are as wide and excited as his voice is reverent and adoring. "Beyond the symbol of weather, she represents feminine leadership and transformation. Very powerful."

I laugh, a little nervous at how much this is getting to Chief. "I don't remember any lightning striking when she arrived."

"This is my point! Lightning did strike, but not you. A third soul was in this agreement."

I shake my head, not getting it.

"A young shaman was in the room when you placed your order. He felt something, so he journeyed to Oya for wisdom. She told him to take the carving for you, to ready it on your behalf. He knew what that meant."

He pauses, no doubt for effect. He's really into this story.

"Well?" I probe.

"The young shaman took the statue, which was ready for you in only a week. He lived with it until Oya said he could send it to you. In that time he lost his house to fire, all his herds of animals to flood, and a sandstorm nearly took his eyesight. He lost his left heel when a tree struck by lightning fell on him. Now he walks with a limp. All for you, Sweet Mary. All so that you could have Oya's power, without the trials she demands of those who call upon her."

"You realize this is going to wreak havoc on my already overworked Catholic guilt complex, don't you? I mean, some guy in Africa has a heel missing, not to mention herds and a house? All so I can call on a wooden goddess icon I just stashed in storage before coming to the reservation?"

Chief looks almost irritated, as least as irritated as I can imagine him. "Guilt is something this shaman knows nothing of. Your guilt existed long before this lifetime, when you chose Catholicism to bring it to the surface. If you told the African it made you feel guilty, he would not understand the word. Nor should you. For what he has done for you, he is now a powerful shaman, even though he is young. He is grateful to you for the opportunity. To him, it was a fair trade."

"You're losing me again, coach. I do nothing, another guy gets creamed, and we both get power? And this is a fair trade?"

Chief smiles and shakes his head. "So much logic in that little head. But it does even out. You took on certain hardships for him in another life. He stepped forward in this one. The great wheel of karma turns—everything is a fair trade, if you trace it back far enough."

"Tell me about this past life when I did something for him. Was I like, a queen, or something?" Something flashes in my mind, something about Dark Crow. I dismiss it. Queenly lives, I can handle. Any life with the likes of Dark Crow, I have the very good sense to avoid.

Chief laughs, a sound as sweet as church bells on a country Christmas morning. "Royal lifetimes are not so important to remember. Others, the ones with pain still buried alive, the ones that remind you of Dark Crow? Those are the ones you will want to revisit, to be on with your task."

He notices the look on my face and smiles. "We will save that for later in the day. For now, some tea?"

Later sounds good, even if only in the day. "Any chance of breakfast? I've lost track, but I'm pretty sure I haven't eaten in quite a while."

"No. I am sorry. Food will not be good for your journeys. Tea is okay."

I don't want to know. Not where we are going, or why it won't be good to eat, or anything to do with anything. Conversing with Chief opens a door onto a whole new world. Several, actually. I'm still back trying to comprehend the Hannah/Puck connection.

"Tea would be great," I say, happy there are still a few simple pleasantries to engage in. In fact, the idea of simple pleasantries after such topics as Oya and guilt sounds very nice. "So, how did you sleep?"

He moves to make the tea, lovingly unwrapping a small leather pouch full of leaves. "I didn't. I haven't slept in ten years," he replies, announcing this unbelievable feat with no more fanfare than a "fine, thank you."

It is tempting bait, but my inquiring mind is already full to the gills. For now, I'm sticking with the small stuff.

"There is no small stuff," he says, reading my mind again. "Not anymore. We are already a decade behind schedule."

16

Chief pours tea into my cup and his own. It seems he is not going to eat either. That concerns me, given his age and severe underweight, but I'm hardly going to try to mother him. Since there is no small stuff, I might as well ask some of the questions I've been dying to.

"Why did Dark Crow agree to bring me here?"

Chief nods, as if affirming the topic. "When he was a small boy, he saw some very bad things. The hardest for him was seeing his father eaten alive by a bear."

"I knew it!" I say with great satisfaction.

Chief nods again, like he expected nothing less. "He was a dark soul, even as a boy. Terrible things that happened to other people did not disturb him. Yet the bear created terrible nightmares. He would wake up sweating every night, several times each night, for many years. The demons in him were awake. They would not let him sleep."

I sit, spellbound to this story, which somehow feels so close to my own, though I cannot say why. I'm not a dreamer and I have never seen anyone eaten by a bear.

Chief shakes his head, obviously seeing in his mind's eye more than I want to imagine. "It was a house of horrors inside his head."

The way he says it, I almost feel sorry for Dark Crow.

"When I came to see Wyunetta Morningstar many years ago," he continues, "to prepare for these days, I knew he would cause trouble. That is his great role in this life, and many others. To purchase his assistance, I wrestled with the dark side on his behalf. Like the shaman in Africa took your calamities, I took the nightmares for Dark Crow. So long as I am alive, he cannot hurt you, or the demons will return ten times as strong. He knows that."

"He told me he'd seen that happen," I say, "but when I asked if he was the boy, he denied it. I doubted my knowing," I look at Chief and smile meekly, "as usual, huh?"

"Yet you did not doubt that the two of you were at war when first you met."

I think back to that first meeting in Wyunetta's hogan, and remember thinking just that. "No, I knew that was true."

"You often know what you know. Hold on to the certain knowings, like templates, to compare to other questions you have. A true knowing feels one way in your stomach. A false one feels another way. When the feelings match, you can act on what you know with confidence. Learn this well. It is the only way for us to accomplish the great mission we have."

I am afraid to ask of the mission, afraid of my part. I remember that I still have an ace in the hole, that I am not The One, but I quickly release the thought, in hopes that Chief will not catch it and dispel my last excuse.

Chief laughs bells again and looks to the cloud-whisked sky. "Now, we get busy. There is work to do."

A flood of relief washes through me. Work to do, not all this deep theory stuff.

"What work is that?"

"A journey," he replies.

With amazing agility, he moves to the canyon wall, eagerly ascending a set of hand and toe holds. Two dozen feet above, he climbs into a darkened space on the wall, a natural inden-tation that is shaded from the sunlight. He disappears, then reappears with a large drum and a hide bundle on his back, and scales down. I watch, open-mouthed. A hundred and eight years old? May I be so healthy at fifty-eight.

Carefully, and with great respect, he lays the bundle on the canyon floor. A medicine bundle. I'd know it anywhere. There's an energy to them that is unmistakable, wherever in the world you are. Power, healing, if not the moon and stars inside. I watch him produce from it a whole host of sacred objects—feathers, stones, a magnificent crystal, a copper bowl, a wad of sage, a turtle shell, some kind of metallic triangular disk, a set of Tibetan bells and a horse-hoof rattle. He draws a circle in the sand I recognize as a medicine wheel. Now we're getting into my territory. I've witnessed a multitude of journeys. Each one has been magical. But what must this shapeshifter be capable of?

When he turns his drum to me, I see it has the exact same markings as the one Wyunetta Morningstar sent to Mary Margaret Begaye of Scottsdale. I knew there was a connection! I still don't know what, but I have a feeling I'm better at this know-what-you-know stuff than I realized. Could the baby mystic be cutting grown-up teeth?

"It is not a question of growing up," Chief comments, "but of remembering what you have always known. Remember who you are, and so reclaim your every innate power."

I nod, willing to entertain any idea that comes from this great man.

With this, he returns his attention to his task, moving swiftly, intently serious, as if he's waited his whole life for this one moment. In the copper bowl he lights some sage and starts waving it around, smoking me. I know the tradition, and willingly submit to it. He may be the one journeying, but all present must be purified. Getting rid of the "bad air" as Maria, my Amazon shaman friend, put it. The whole ceremony centers the intentions of those present, setting the stage for a powerful journey.

I watch Chief smoke himself with dramatic, elegant sweeps, like a confident woman perfumes herself for a long-awaited lover. In all my studies, in all my experiences, I have never seen such reverence as this. It makes me wonder what deals he has made and with which gods and goddesses? It sets my own excitement at high throttle. God, I wish I had paper and a pen to document this one.

Where will he go? The Underworld? The Upper Worlds? What will be his intent? Information? Some kind of blessing? How long will he be gone? What will he ask of me as he goes?

A fear overtakes me. Am I to drum? I don't know how, though I could probably muddle along. Will he ask me to chant some sacred song? I know several by heart. But I never have actually done it. My job, always, no matter who the shaman or what part of the world, has been to be the unobtrusive witness, to learn by watching and judge as little as possible. I have not even dared participate in healings, for fear of losing my objectivity. Now, with so much witnessing and so little participation, I feel impotent for anything but mere observation.

Chief stops abruptly. "You do not understand. I am no longer able to journey. It is long past my time here on earth. The other worlds would keep me if I left my body now. It is you who will journey today, Sweet Mary."

"Oh no," I say, "no, no, no." I shake my head again and again, pulling out my standard-issue refusal as I have so many times. "I'm sorry, but I've made it a policy, as a social scientist, never to actually get involved in such journeying. It is important in my line of work to remain as neutral an observer as...."

"I know," he replies flatly, again attending to his ceremonial preparations, "that your role as scientific witness is a smoke-screen, one the whole Western world uses whenever it is afraid. Behind your smoke is an unworthiness I do not accept. Now, for your instruction."

17

Chief has given me detailed instruction, but I have only half listened. He hit the hammer on the head. Me, worthy to journey? Who am I to meet the Otherworld? I swear, for God's sake, and have scars across my knuckles from Sister Agatha, Sister Sue, and all the other sisters at St. Agnes to prove it. Do the gods want me traveling the ethereal terrain, with my foul mouth and eternal skepticism? No, it is out of respect for the other worlds that I have kept myself here on the earthly plane.

This time, it appears, I'm not going to get out of it.

"Mary!" Chief implores, then sighs. "Ah, well, it is nothing you do not already know. You will remember what you need to."

He goes about his ceremony while I try to recall the aspects of his instructions that I did retain. I am to put my left wrist on my forehead and lie flat on my back, right arm to my side. Once he has finished with his chanting, facing the four directions and requesting assistance via rattling and prayer, he will begin drumming. At which point I am to "become one" with the drum until I am "walking between the beats." Like I know what that means. I can't even keep the beat when dancing.

Assuming I get this far, the beat will carry me off, and I am to then look for guides to help me, probably animals, but maybe not. Then, I am to request to see the Keeper of All Records, ask for information on finding something called "The Essence Of Ray," then return when the drum beat begins in double-time. Piece of cake. Nothing more than a short hop to the grocery for a few items to get you through the week.

Right.

"You must return," Chief emphasizes again. Like I'm gonna stay somewhere I don't want to go in the first place?

It sounds easy enough, but fear rolls around my gut like a can opener's beveled slice. All to bring forth the pork and beans of me and my woefully inadequate psyche. I want to throw up, now understanding the value in not eating. Maybe Chief knows what he is doing, after all. Not that I doubted him. It's me I doubt. Always me.

As Chief rattles to the wind in reverence, I can't help but focus on what I will find, inside. Is it the mess I suspect? Answers to questions I don't want? I've avoided looking my whole life, looking instead at the pork and beans of others, helping them when I could. The common cry "what about me?" is one I have not dared think, let alone throw out into the universe. I have not wanted to know. The answer always seemed too big and dark, shadowed by something I have long felt yet never understood. Now perhaps I will, assuming I am able to stand the looking, and the sorting, and the making sense of it all.

Lifting corn pollen to the sky, Chief declares his intent to honor our hosts, the Navajo gods and goddesses. Then, in Navajo, he chants, sounding completely authentic, even in his glottal stops. So much so, I'd swear he was born and raised here, though he has said otherwise. Where does this man come from?

His chanting complete, Chief indicates he is ready with a nod. Resigned, I return the nod, finding my position on the dirt floor of the canyon. The low, resonant tones of tightly pulled deer skin begin, close to that of my own heartbeat.

My fears dance throughout my body as the drumming finds its way into my arms, legs, even the wrist upon my forehead, as if my molecules are speeding up, ready to go somewhere. I worry about using my imagination in this. I have been told by many different shamans that the imagination is the portal Spirit must use to communicate ideas through. But I'm not exactly experienced in using it for anything, given my strong preference for nuts and bolts.

Readiness, too, is an issue in question. Didn't shamans wait years and years, with much guidance and training, to take such journeys? Would the Spirits not frown upon such unprepared visits? Or worse, laugh me back to my proper place? My only comfort is that Chief believes it is a worthy endeavor. I trust him, much more than I trust myself.

Just get to the task at hand, you chicken.

I focus on what is around me, a trick I was told by a powerful Australian shaman. The dirt below, hard. The feel of Wyunetta Morningstar's velvet shirt sleeve edging between my wrist and forehead, soft. The rustle of wind, caressing. The drum, loud, beginning to seduce me out of my mind, into my senses.

I remember Chief said to look for a portal to the under-world, a hole in the ground or in the base of a tree. Without warning, I remember a tree whose roots were showing at the side of a creek that had receded. Hannah and I went there when we were kids. I see it. Can I go down from here?

All at once, I'm in it.

I'm nowhere, between worlds, yet going somewhere. Down, it feels, and then across. There is nothing but the dark-ness of my eyelids, so no markers can be offering this sensa-tion. I see nothing, and yet something, perhaps the vast empty tombs of my mind. They feel hollow, as if abandoned long ago.

The pungent earth meets my nostrils, or at least the nostrils in my mind. The deep tones of the drum begin to grow fainter. It is not the beat that is changed, I realize, but more a sense of my moving farther and farther away from it.

Amazing. The idea makes me feel giddy, like riding my first roller coaster, taking that first deep drop, and being okay after all.

Would there be guides? Immediately a mountain lion appears on my left, fierce and muscled, yet seeming a helper. She is huge, the alpha female, moving with profound intent.

How funny to be in the Lion's Mouth, with a lion beside me. I feel a smile on my face, the face I have left up there, in the middle world, next to Chief.

I also feel distant from it, separate from my own smile. Is this how it works? One foot in two worlds? Yet I cannot sustain the question. It, like the drum, seems to fade from me, unim-portant. I let go. Perhaps for the first time in my life, it feels okay, even safe, to be in my own self.

"You're doing fine," Lion says without words. More telepathy. Here, in my dreaming world, it seems more reasonable than up there, in real time.

"Do I know you?" I ask, thinking maybe I do.

Her head dips in affirmation. "We are old friends."

I wonder, in the Native American lore, what the mountain lion is said to represent. Yet it seems ridiculous to me that I might be questioning how any tradition would interpret the spirit of the lion, when a lion is here with me, able to speak.

"Good," she says, sounding pleased indeed. "It is your task to put aside the ideas of any other, even an entire culture, to know what you know."

I think of Chief and knowing what I know. Something here feels very right. My stomach is now calm, I notice, and the rest of me too. I am safe as the witness, witnessing me. Yet it is not a sensation of being drawn up and away, as it is when I become the bird, looking down. More, it is a going within, looking even deeper inside.

"What do you represent, then?" I ask.

"I am that which is fearless within you. When you walked into the canyon, and into my mouth, you walked into your own fearlessness. We have waited a long time for you."

I want to ask who "we" is, but I notice myself pulling even farther away from my body, as if departing from it. It is such an odd feeling, it distracts me.

Lion points a way further down, through another set of tree roots. "Kenya is eager to meet with you."

I know Kenya is the Keeper of Records I am to find, though I have no rational reason to know this. "She knows I am coming?"

"Kenya has access to all knowledge," Lion tells me. "Past, present, and all possible futures." I feel no need to question this, though up there, in my rational mind and body, I would have doubted, called it hokey. Again I smile, but this time I cannot feel my lips move on my real face. Perhaps it is my heart that smiles. I begin to feel giddy again, floating on a stream of brightly colored ribbons. Gliding into my true self.

This stops me short. I feel my physical body jerk. I'm not ready to see my true self. Not yet. It's too much. The drumming is loud again. I have lost my way. Of course. Who was I to think I could do this so easily? Me, ever too uptight.

"Shhh..." I hear Chief say as the drumming continues uninterrupted.

It reminds me of his warning that this might occur, especially in my first journeys. I remember his instructions to humbly begin again, listening to the drum. I do.

Thump, thump, thump....

In no time, I find Lion. She has waited.

"It's a brave thing you are doing," she says to me. It comforts me, draws me out of my self-recrimination for having let myself get lost. It strikes me this must be a guide's greatest task. I swell with admiration for Lion. Surely she can teach me about fearlessness.

"Can I set limits on this?" I ask her. "There are some things I know I am not ready for."

"This is your life. We are only guides, though you may be ready for more than you believe."

"We?" I ask.

As if in answer, I find myself in a huge forest of gigantic trees, vivid in color and shape. She motions with her head for me to turn around.

I do, and see a host of animals. A swan, a moose and a salamander are at the forefront. Behind them, dozens of tall pillars of light, illuminated brightly from within, emitting a glow ten times that of Chief, yet it does not overly brighten the Underworld. Surrounding us are trees, alive and animated. For the first time, I see them for what they are—gift givers, oxygen providers, spirit beings as shapeshifters in their own right.

I know I am sucked in now. Yet it seems so real.

In unison, this heavenly crowd bows to me, sending not mere chills, but bolts of electricity rolling up and down my spine. I am at once delighted, honored and embarrassed. I wonder what this means, that in my imagination I would create columns of light and animal spirits and massive trees to bow to me, if in fact the imagination is all this is.

The drumming becomes louder again. I connect the dots to this cause and effect: When I question what I see, I lose my ability to see at all. I relax, return to Lion. She suggests I put such thoughts into a balloon and let them gently float away. I do.

The group before me once again becomes clear. I accept their adulation reluctantly, returning their bow in thanks and reverence.

"We have arrived," Lion says. I turn to see a cave-like structure and a door. "Go on, Mary. You are walking between the drum beats now."

18

I am not sure how I got to walking between the drum beats, but I trust that I am where I am supposed to be. Before me, the cave door begins to open. Once inside, it closes behind me, hemming me into a small room. At least it feels small. I find myself in pitch dark. Whether it is the darkness of my psyche or someplace more real, I do not know. A door on the other side opens to a warm, candlelit room that smells of oily lemon and heavy saffron.

"Welcome, I am Kenya," a woman says, her voice steeped in African influence. "It has been so long."

She extends her long, slender arms to embrace me, like we are old friends. I hesitate, not being the hugging type, even here in the Underworld. She quickly changes her stance to offer her hand. I offer mine readily. "Of course, you don't remember," she says with compassion.

"Have we met before?" I ask, my eyes adjusting to the light.

"In the beginning," she says, as if that should mean something to me. I smile politely.

"I'll just be a minute," she says, turning gracefully and moving to her kitchen. She begins making tea. I take the opportunity to look her over.

She appears human, and yet not quite, as if she is something between a flesh-and-blood woman and a spirit. Her skin is as black as I've seen, with an odd texture, like that of construction paper. She seems larger than life, though her size is no greater than my own. Perhaps there is simply more of her to her, more of who she is in who she is. Yes, that seems to be it.

Her clothes, patterned in swirls of bright red, yellow, orange and rich browns, sway with her thin upper body and padded hips. There is enough fabric to give it a flowing look, yet one arm remains uncovered, creating a sultry image I'd die to be able to pull off—at least for the right lover.

The spool-like necklace of more than a dozen rows of small black, white and brown wooden beads covers the full of what must be at least eight inches of slender neck, adding to her dark sensuality. She reaches to fill a sugar bowl. The dozens of fine gold bracelets adorning her upper arms, caught between her armpits and small but firm triceps, tinkle like chimes.

Her jet black hair is cut so short it gives the illusion of her head being shaved. You can see the contours of her huge skull which seems to hang too far over the back of her neck. Strange. Enchanting. A princess of some kind, I think, were she fully real. Maybe a goddess, from the same neck of the woods as Oya even.

Who says you have no imagination, Mary Margaret Hathaway?

Finished with her task, a tray of tea in her hands, she nods delicately, inviting me to sit. I find my seat on one of many huge, overstuffed chairs, perfectly matched to her outfit. I sink into comfort, amazed at how real it feels to my skin, which I know is really somewhere else, up there, on a bed of canyon sand. I notice the drumming, but I am not at all interested in returning, and so readily let it fade.

"Tea?" she suggests. Then, hearing me chuckle, asks: "Is something funny?"

"It just seems strange, that you would have tea here. It's such a physical thing to do, yet you are so...metaphysical."

She laughs a melody. "If you can imagine you are here, is it so hard to imagine enjoying tea?"

"I guess not."

She offers me a dark, steaming, oversized cup. It tastes of hickory smoke and yet smells of something odd, a strange blend that I can't recall experiencing in my life up there, where Chief is. In the far distance I hear the drumming again, yet this time it is no more distracting than my own heartbeat. Whatever is happening, I am truly both here and there. In a flash, I catch a glimpse of how Chief might shapeshift. The insight is fleeting.

"How is Chief?" she asks me.

"Good. He sends his affections," I say, remembering now that he had made the request.

Her face takes on a slightly crimson glow in response. Only now do I register that a similar glow had occurred on his face when he'd mentioned her. If she were fully human, I'd bet my entire crystal collection they'd been lovers. But the age difference?

"He always came to me as a young man," Kenya says, another who knows my thoughts. "A warrior. He knew how I loved that archetype. Very strong, manly, eager to win me. Even the last time, when he was living out a human form of almost a hundred, he appeared as a twenty-year-old." She sighs a sigh of loving reminisce. "Tell him I miss him."

"Why doesn't he come anymore?" I ask, fully able to imagine him as she has described.

"He hasn't told you much," she says, a statement more than a question, setting down her tea. Her tone is sad, almost as if she pities me.

"Truthfully," I say, feeling a bit as if I ought to defend my Chief, "I haven't been the most willing student."

She smiles. "It's a lot to take in."

"Are you and Chief soul mates?" The question had only begun to form in my mind when it was out of my mouth.

Kenya laughs, and the music fills the chamber, like an organ suddenly piping out sweet high notes. "Goodness, no. My soul mate is a hundred galaxies away. Chief really ought to have told you more by now. But are you sure you have not guessed?"

On an intuitive level, I feel I have again hit onto an area I don't want to understand yet. I take what I feel might be a juicy detour.

"Do you mean you and Chief had an illicit affair?"

She laughs again, hearty and delicate all at once.

"Tell me, do you like chocolate ice cream?"

"Yes."

"Do you like strawberry?"

"Yes," I answer again, wondering where this is leading.

"I tell you this, Mary, there will come a day when you will have no more of a moral dilemma choosing mating partners than you do choosing ice cream. There will be love enough to share with any and all."

"What?!"

"It is true. A day will come when you will realize that security is an illusion, there is no such thing, and no such thing as a need for it. You will not need to deny yourself any relationship with any soul to protect the security of another relationship. Chocolate will revel in being chocolate, and be enjoyed by whomever loves chocolate. Chocolate will not fear it has no one to love it, just because someone who usually chooses chocolate decides to spend an evening with strawberry."

"Ice cream and sexual partners are hardly the same," I argue. "No offense, but are you sure you know much about us humans?"

Her face grows sad. "Too much, especially the humans in your so-called developed world. They live in great and constant fear. They have everything and more, yet they fear not having enough to consider themselves worthy, and when they have enough, they fear losing it. They fear change, imagining they can hold it back if they stick to their routines. Like a dam holding back the constant influx of water, they live in a security they do not need, then cry out as the floods come, bringing all the change at once. Which is, I admit, quite a shock. They don't understand how it all works, but they will. You've come to help them."

"Good God, I hope the message of The One isn't free sex," I say, knowing for sure they have the wrong girl if it is. I like to think I'm pretty open about sex, especially given my upbringing. In reality, though, I'm probably still a little too uptight.

"Not at all," Kenya says reassuringly, "you simply asked about my relationship with Chief. Yes, I have been his lover. As has Oya, and many of the other goddesses. He is the essence of love, why wouldn't we? But this extends far beyond sexual choice or actions."

You dog, Chief! No wonder you got so excited when you were telling me about Oya. It's pretty hard to imagine, but then, I am talking to a big-skulled blacker-than-black cave woman. Where am I supposed to draw the line?

Kenya looks at me with penetrating eyes. "With your help, fear is going to leave the earth pattern, sooner than you think. When it does, all the rules and regulations about sex, and many other taboos, will seem as pointless as outlawing strawberry ice cream might seem to you now. Of course, deep commitment for the sake of that kind of learning will still be chosen more often than not, but it will not be a moral choice."

I lean forward, putting my tea in its saucer and looking straight back into the brown saucers of Kenya's eyes. "This change, not about sex, but about fear. Are you sure it is coming?"

"I am sure. It is the earth plan. It always has been."

I sit back with pointed conviction. "Then why does it matter if The One plays this part? Who needs her?"

"You, Mary," she says, looking at me in all earnest, "are the variable we are all holding our breath on. A pendulum is swinging, a time for change is ripe. You, depending on how much courage you have, will determine if this fearless state has a chance to come soon, very soon. Or, if it must wait for another chance very, very, very far into the future."

I let out a deep breath. "Well, I don't know. I mean, what do you say to something like that?"

"Why, say 'yes,' of course," she replies with simplistic enthusiasm. Her eyes grow seriously majestic as she continues. "What else does God say to God's plan?"

19

I am saved by the doorbell, a deep tone that Kenya excuses herself to answer.

It gives me a moment to prepare an excuse.

I mean, me? God? Well, sure, in theory. I can accept that we all have a spark of divinity in us. But still, it's pretty egocentric to actually say, "I'm God, and I'm saying yes to My plan, which I've chosen me to be The One for."

Anyway, where does that leave everyone else? You don't see people lining up out there claiming to be The One. Why is it I'm bestowed this privilege? Something just doesn't mesh. But no matter. I'm not The One anyway. All Kenya has to do is look wherever she looks for information to find that out.

At the door, I notice two very large men—more like humpback thugs, actually—bending down to speak to Kenya. Their voices are baritone. I can only make out a few words..."eager for a change" and "playing by the rim" and "falling." Kenya instructs them in words I suspect she intends me to hear.

"I'll put a bird's feather in his way about ten minutes ago. That will distract him while I do a small time jump."

She pauses for a moment, then continues. "Don't forget to appear to him as angels. He likes angels. Tell him changes are coming, but it is not yet time. Oh, yes, and remind him he is brave."

They nod and she closes the door, returning to sit with me, sipping her tea. We sit in silence, until I can't stand it anymore.

"Don't you have to do something, with a feather?" I ask hesitantly.

"I'm doing it," she replies matter-of-factly, turning her head to give me a side view. The veins pulse and move, like ants scurrying around inside a huge, tender gourd.

"That is...interesting."

"It's all telepathy, at this point. Of course, I had to learn using more tangible tools. Like you, I wanted to see it all. Proof for my logical side. Now I simply think it in here," she points again to the throbbing mass, "and it occurs in your world, up there."

"I wouldn't mind learning that trick," I say with a laugh.

"Well, why not? It would take quite some time to teach you how my brain works. But I can show you how it works using the manual method. That's the way I first learned. If you like, that is."

If I like? She's going to change the past and she wants to know if I'd like to see how? "I'd love it."

She sets down her tea and leads me to a darkened window.

"It's so archaic, it's almost embarrassing," she says.

As if we are sitting on the side of the earth, she opens the window out onto a galaxy of space—in front of us, instead of above. A million stars and planets seem within touching distance.

"Here, let's turn up the sound."

However archaic she feels it is, I can see she's still delighted to share her toy with me.

Music pours out of the window, a choir sounding something like crickets, only instead of chirping, they seem to be laughing. A symphony of harmonic sound begins, clearer and more intricate than anything any I've heard before. Strange instruments create sounds I've never imagined. It is as if what we call a full orchestra up there is a mere quartet by comparison. All this in the bulb of one head?

Carefully her hands bring forth one star out of the millions. As it comes closer, it grows nearly a foot in circumference. I remind myself that I am on a journey within my own psyche, that this is all coming from inside me, using my imagination. It seems impossible. For the first time, I begin to realize what the Masters have long said may be true—that all the answers are inside each of us.

"This," she sweeps her arm to encompass the huge galaxy we are a witness to, "is really only a parable. You must realize that."

A parable? I don't understand, but am willing to imagine understanding.

The star she has pulled forth, careful as a surgeon, becomes less a ball of light and more like a living, breathing geometric light form. It seems to be made of tiny, intricate patterns of metal bars, the width of a hair. Amazing crystal formations have grown on each one. The patterns are beautiful—beyond beautiful. They are pure art.

As Kenya pulls it even closer, it continues to grow, as if there were a microscope bringing it into focus. Stunning beauty. And, oh, the sound! It stirs me to tears, so innocent and pure, yet happy, as if it is delighted with itself.

"What I did in my head was a kind of micro-surgery, implanting a chip of crystal on this bar, which translates to a beautiful yellow and black feather, bringing our boy some pleasure to keep him from making his way to the canyon wall again."

I nod, amazed. My face must register it, because she laughs, then takes my hand. "Here," she says, moving my hand into the space surrounding this particular star. "Be careful not to touch the structure itself," she warns. "How does it feel to you?"

The electricity is amazing, and the tears begin to flow in silent torrents, as if my tear ducts were a natural spring. "Like I'm touching God," I say.

"Yes. Does it feel like anyone you know?"

"Anyone? A person?" She nods. I try to match it. Alive, pulsating music fills my brain, seems almost to enter into my hands. Like touching life. But what kind of life? Exuberant and precious, full of soul, excited.

"Yes! I know this feeling! It is the feeling I got when I was with Hannah. And again, when I was with Puck!"

"Yes," Kenya says, looking proud of me.

I bask for a moment in the wonder of it all, then suddenly remember why we are doing this. Puck must be the one in trouble. "You mean Puck is playing at the edge of the canyon? He's in danger of falling?" I feel the danger rip at my heart. "Are you sure you can help him?" I am instantly panicked, unwilling, unable to fathom losing this great soul again so young.

"It's already done. My staff got to him before he landed. It's a common occurrence with that one, so they watch him pretty carefully and know how to get to him in a hurry."

"Why is it so common?"

"He's susceptible, in part because life is so hard now, and in part because he is accustomed to dying young. He's just feeling a little desperate for a change."

My eyes fly open wide. "You don't mean he is trying to kill himself!"

Kenya puts a gentle hand on my shoulder. "Not consciously, of course, but his lack of hope has affected his survival instinct, and his reflexes are slow because of it. Unfortunately, I can't put in the transfer request immediately, as it depends on...other things. All I can do is help him hold on a little while longer."

I shake my head repeatedly, unconvinced. "I don't like it."

"He is just fine. A visit from the angels will tide him over, I am sure, until a better home is ready."

"What is wrong with his current home?" I ask, defensive, thinking again of parents who would tell him that he bores them with his questions.

The wince of her eyes tells me too much. I remember the scars on his back. A sick feeling comes over me, the same one that came when they told me about Hannah.

"Oh, Kenya, no. Can't you get him out of there? Right now?" With my hand still in his energy field, my heart seems to now be experiencing his bewilderment, his terror.

"We are working on it," Kenya says softly.

"Well you're not working on it fast enough!" I tear my eyes away from her, feeling betrayed.

An anger I know all too well swells in me. It is deep-seated and pointed directly at God, or whatever Powers That Be, for letting such atrocities go on, for creating humans capable of such madness.

"Let him come to me, to my life, then. I'll take him. I'll make a life for him. Just flip a switch for us both. Now!"

Kenya carefully pulls my shaking hand from the sweet Hannah/Puck energy, unplugging me somewhere deep inside. The anger rushes out as my knees give way. I crumple to the floor, feeling death come over me again. I remember this loss, this evaporation of spirit that was once in my life. Again, I am powerless to do anything about it.

Kenya's voice is firm. "You cannot let this get in the way of your destiny. Puck's soul has put in a transfer request. That is all he needs to do. It will take a little time. But when anyone decides that the current reality they are experiencing is no longer their true choice, and most important, begins to dream of a new way of life, I am required to make a change."

"But how can I stand by and do nothing?"

"You have already done what is most important. You showed him what it feels like to be accepted for who he is. Now that he knows what kind of love is possible, he has really begun to dream of it for himself. There is no power that can stop dreams like that. Not when they are repeated in the imagination again and again. You have been the catalyst for Puck."

"But that's not enough. Kenya, please, I could give him a home," I say, fully able to imagine how incredible that would be. Hang my vow not to have children. The vow was made for the very one who needs me. "It's not like I'm doing anything else with my life."

"Is that so?" Kenya challenges, lifting me from the floor and moving me back to a chair, picking up a stack of papers on her way. "Look here. Look at all these transfer requests. New dreams, all because of you."

I look at a large pile of geometric symbols, one to a page. They mean nothing to me.

"Six children last week started dreaming about going to college, because you talked to them about it when you read to them in the bookmobile. Eric, your friend, has begun to dream about having a woman like you in his life, to help bring him back to what really matters. Jimmy Two Feathers has ordered more crystals for his store and is reading about them so he can help educate his customers, instead of simply playing his usual 'con the tourist' game. All that dreaming turns into all these transfer requests."

I shrug, unconvinced this is any great feat next to a child who needs me.

"Here," she says, pulling out another paper. "This is for the young woman on Nelson's tour, the one who will one day get throat cancer, as you saw. You prayed for her—and how very easy it is to make a change with that kind of power behind a request! Because of your example, and your prayer, now she's dreaming of being courageous, like the woman she saw hiking off into the canyon on her own. That is something this young woman would never have done without your example.

"To get that kind of courage, she will have to face death's door, as you knew. She doesn't realize that she put in the transfer to get sick sooner rather than later in life, but that will do it."

Kenya continues shuffling through her stack of papers. "Even Wyunetta Morningstar, here. She's ready to die now, because her dream of seeing you again has come to pass at last."

I cannot utter a word, not even to ask if that makes me responsible for Wyunetta's death, though the thought throws a stone into my heart.

"You blow into and out of lives, Mary, never knowing how you make a difference. You, by nature of who you are, cannot exist without being this catalyst. It is the essence of you. Even before you have accepted your role as The One. All these requests, all these dreams which must come true, simply by you being yourself."

I cannot think what to say, how to feel. I cling to my last defense, my only loophole, the one fact I have to get myself out of this great responsibility.

"I am not who you say I am," I say flatly.

"Of course you are. Do you think I would not know?"

I want to believe her. Who wouldn't? But I am resolute to have the truth out there, finally and for good. "No. I thought I might be, but Wyunetta was wrong. I never nursed at her breast. Just consider her age, and my skin color."

I sigh, knowing that the gig is finally up. I am relieved to say it, once and for all, though I know when I am done, when I am back up there and it is all over, I will wish I had been who they wanted me to be. Maybe then I could have saved Puck, and helped more of the Pucks of the world.

"Yes," she answers, gently but with insistence. "Wyunetta is old. Old enough to have birthed you a lifetime ago."

"What are you saying?" I ask, feeling as if I know, that I just need to be told to connect the dots I have long been afraid to connect. I put my hand on my heart to keep it from breaking out of my chest, like a racehorse at the gate.

"It was almost fifty years ago," she explains. "You only lived six months before a fever took you. It ought not have, but you had little interest in being incarnated. 'Failure to thrive' is what they would call it today. After her only daughter died, the woman you knew to call your Great Mother begged the Divine, day after day, to see her only daughter one more time. In this lifetime. An unusual request, but your Great Mother was an unusual woman."

I listen, my hand now on my stomach. At my center, deep inside, it tells me all of this is true.

"Your Great Mother imagined it happening, somehow, every day, day after day. She banged on the Divine's door again and again, insisting, dreaming and believing. With that kind of prayer, which the Divine loves and does hear, even you could not escape being fed by your Great Mother one more time."

I sink into the chair, feeling as if my world has shattered. Love has broken it, broken in. Everything I have known of who I am is changed. I am not only the daughter of a fourteen-year-old girl who didn't want me, even when she grew up. I am also the daughter of a great woman, a Great Mother who loved me enough to bang on the door of the Divine repeatedly until she got what she longed for. A simple meal with me.

Everything I know of myself, my unworthiness, recedes as a ray of light beams into my heart, opening it up. At once, and at last, I believe that it might be true. Maybe I am The One they have been waiting for. Maybe, just maybe, I am here to help change the world as I have long dreamed.

The Divine, it seems, has heard my banging, too.

20

A part of me wants to bask in my newfound knowledge, the idea that I may be The One, that my life might yet prove to have the kind of meaning I have hoped for. Another part of me wants to understand the logistics. The what, where, when and why of it all.

"What is The One here to do?" I ask.

Kenya shakes her head. "Not yet, Mary. There are many other journeys to take, more revelations to come. You cannot know what you intend to do until you know who you really are."

"How do I learn that?"

"First, you must understand why you failed to thrive in your last life."

"Can't you just tell me?"

"Also the difficulties you encountered in the life before that. In fact, you'll have to work your way back to where it all began, where you first sold your soul."

This surprises me even more than the news of my Great Mother. "Me? Sell my soul? I never sell out. Not for materialism, not for anything. Half the time, that's what gets me in so much trouble."

Kenya nods as if to say she understands my point of view, yet I don't feel she is conceding hers. "All humans sell their soul in one way or another. Parts of it, little bits here and there along the way. Of course, there is always the chance to buy it back. Nothing is solid. Certainly not the past."

I don't know what to say, to think.

Again I am saved by the bell. Kenya gets up to answer the door. The two big guys are there again. This time I hear them clearly, as if they are trying to be heard.

"The boy is fine," the first one says.

"He asked us 'angels' to please find out if Mary knows she is The One yet," the second one adds.

Kenya turns to look at me and raises her eyebrows. "Well?"

All three of them stare at me as if the fate of the world were hinging on my answer. Images of selling my soul crowd my mind, as does the idea of buying it back. Maybe, with my soul returned, I could be what Puck needs me to be, and all the other Pucks I've met. The young prostitutes in Haiti, the mortar-carrying children in India. All drowning in Nothin', just like me.

"Yes," I say, before I've even decided to answer. Chills ripple through my body, as if someone threw a boulder into the stagnant lake that is me and everything had to wake up.

The men leave without another word. Kenya sits close to me, putting her hand around my shoulder. "It's a very great thing you just did," she says. "You are braver than you realize. There is so much you must now remember, so many lifetimes that still have an impact on today. You'll need to journey to them, as you have come to me."

I swallow and do not speak.

"It will be like rebreaking bones that have not set right. You will have to own up to some very painful truths. There is danger in that process, but there is also power in the vision you have held all your life, to help this world. The vision is your destiny, and it will pull you toward it."

I am fully able to imagine this terrible rebreaking of bones. The thought makes me sick to my stomach. Even so, the vision empowers me, the hope of healing and wholeness on the other side of the pain, not only for me, but the broken world I want to aid. I nod slowly.

From above, I again hear Chief's drumming, now in double-time.

"It was good to see you," Kenya says.

"Wait," I reply, suddenly panicked, questions popping up out of nowhere, all at once. So much I need to know before I start. Who is Chief, really? What will she do to help Puck? And Great Mother...will she really die now that I have seen her, and does that mean I am the cause of her death? Can I stop it?

"Wait, wait," I cry, grasping at any straw that will work. "I was supposed to learn about the Essence of Ray. Chief told me to. I can't fail him!"

"You will learn all you need to in your next journeys," Kenya replies.

Above, the drumming becomes insistent. I feel myself going toward the front door, see it open. Lion is here, looking impatient, as if there is some hurry to my return. Why now, when we have had such a leisurely pace?

"It has been so good to see you, Mary," Kenya says.

"But, wait," I say again, too many thoughts crowding my mind. I want more of her wisdom. More of her knowledge. I want to know more about how it works, how it all works. Life. Love. Relationships. How does she turn back time? Make changes? Who is the Divine, anyway? God? What does God think of all this mess we've made of earth?

The drumming grows more and more insistent, driving away at my eardrums, until my head throbs in unison. I feel Chief has moved the drum closer to my head, up there.

I need something more to return with. "Just tell me this. If God wanted to give me one piece of advice, one thing to help me on this quest, what would it be?"

"That you know you are God," Kenya answers.

With that I am swiftly, if not frantically, carried on Lion's powerful back. I feel a swooshing up, back to the surface of life, where I open my eyes to see Chief's drum is only inches from my ear. I shake as if startled. I am fully awake, fully returned to my body, my eyes squinting in the bright sunlight, looking into Chief's glowing face.

"You didn't want to come back," he says.

"I had so many questions I did not get to." I am truly disappointed. "But it was amazing." "Good," he says, glowing with love and maybe, if I am right, even admiration. "Now go over your journey in your mind, again and again. Try to remember everything you can before it slips back into your subconscious. You will lose some of it, naturally, as this was your first time."

Not wanting to forget one moment, I go over every memory still with me. I remember Lion. I remember earthy colors and a comfortable chair. I remember Puck being in trouble, and Kenya making changes in a galaxy within her skull. But most of all, I remember that I was the daughter of Wyunetta Morningstar a lifetime ago and that I may well be, as they have all said, The One.

Chief nods, as if he has been listening in on my recall. "Now that you understand you are who you are, we can progress in our work."

"I'm sorry I doubted you," I say in earnest.

"You weren't doubting me," he assured, "you were doubting you."

I laugh. "But you said we are one, and Kenya said I am God, so I really doubted the whole blessed universe and everyone in charge."

"That," he says, pointing to a waiting cup of water, "is the most profound truth you have spoken."

"Now, though, I've seen the light!" I say, laughing, feeling giddy, at the summit of my own internal quest. I am The One, a woman with a mother—which must mean I am also a sister to Jimmy Two Feathers, my first guide on this quest!—and a student of an old-school skinwalker. It's all too much, too perfect.

Chief laughs. "You will doubt it again, soon enough."

The thought sobers me. He's right, of course. My brain will kick in. I can feel it already. The whole journey took place in my imagination, after all. If I know me, my straight-shooter self will dissect this dream all to hell. Gone. Poof.

"So then what do I do?"

"What everyone must do when they play Shoot The Moon. Risk everything you have and jump into the void."

"The darkness of Nothin'," I say, already resigning myself.

Chief responds with his whole body, his voice full of passion. "No! No! The womb of all possibility, where hope can be birthed, again and again!"

21

I do not share Chief's enthusiasm for the "void." But indulging in the idea of having a true Great Mother is a sweet seduction, only matched by the incredible notion that Puck is Hannah and Chief is a shapeshifter here to aid me in my quest as The One. Like lullabies, the possibilities soothe my analytical brain.

"Kenya said I would be taking other journeys. I'm ready when you are."

Chief's eyes reflect my own excitement. "Soon enough. There is much for you to assimilate."

He looks to the open sky, as if the answers are there, and returns his gaze to me. "We are running out of time. There is still so far to go. Perhaps a bath in the stream by the sacred waterfall would be a refreshment to you, while I take care of speeding things up."

The idea of running out of time and a leisurely bath do not compute, but more and more, I trust Chief to know what we both are doing. I look at his clean cotton attire, and then my own body, covered in a film of red canyon dirt, and have to agree it's a good idea. When I ask how to get there, he simply points me further into the canyon.

"How far?" I ask.

"A ways," he replies.

I'll guess I'll just listen for the waterfall.

"You won't hear it," he replies to my thoughts. "The water only falls when it rains."

"I'm supposed to take a bath in a *dry* waterfall?"

"The water flows by natural spring in the creek below. You can take some water bottles to fill while you are there."

"Right," I say, wondering if a sacred waterfall is still sacred when the water isn't falling. I'd ask, but I'm trying to know what I know. I get up to make my way through the path of thicket, the jutting canyon walls getting closer and closer together the further in I look. I sigh, already thinking lions and bears, vertigo and tricksters.

"If you see a rattler?" Chief says in half-question.

I shoot him a "thanks a lot" look.

He smiles. "It will be a good sign. Snakes mean change is coming."

"Yeah, well, so long as 'dead' is not the change we are looking for."

"Soon enough," he replies to my sarcasm with earnest, "you will see how good dead is."

I sigh again and shake my head. There is no talking to this man without opening one hornet nest upon another. I head off into the canyon, afraid every odd stick is a snake in waiting. Nothing like priming the senses, making one aware of every little crackle beneath the moccasins.

Despite my fear, the walk does me good, gets me back into the land and out of my head. After meeting Kenya, I have to wonder if anything is real. Is it an illusion, as so many mystics say? Is this simply my dream, folding in on itself? Is it all whipped up for the moment I see it, only to disappear again once my back is turned?

The waterfall leads me to itself without effort. God knows how many feet up, I see a wide groove at the top of the canyon wall, as though two walls met by surprise and, over the years, decided to become one. Though the waterfall is dry now, this is Arizona's version of Asia's monsoon season. It could be flowing full force in less than half an hour, should the rain gods so desire. I'm half-tempted to call on Oya, my own personal goddess of weather, just to see if I've really got any sway with her. The idea gives me a bad feeling, like playing with fire at a gas station.

I resign myself to wading less than knee-deep in the cool stream below. The water is clear and fresh, offering me a personal clarity so strong it makes me believe there might really be something especially sacred here. I am too self-conscious to undress, but serene enough to lie on my back and soak myself to the bone. The water washes away the weariness. Looking up at the waterfall ridge, I lose myself. The cool flow of wetness under me, the great canyon walls, the sky going on forever.

I find myself becoming the bird, traveling the canyon at will, losing time until at last I feel ready to return. Quietly, and with a step as tender as Chief's when he carries wood, I wring my clothes of the excess water and begin walking back.

By the time I reach our homestead, there is a bounce in my step. I'm refreshed to the core, ready to work, to rebreak bones and set the world straight. I can't wait to tell Chief how wonderful I feel.

He does not even notice my return.

His agitated walk and wildly waving arms startle me, and the gravity of his face is a shock. It is hard to imagine what might have occurred. He walks heavily and the respect that came into my footfall is gone from his. He tosses branches into the fire without a thought, groaning as he moves, as if for the first time feeling his hundred-and-eight years. In fact, for the first time, he looks his age.

"Chief?" I ask gingerly.

He looks up, a bold agitation in his eyes, something I could never have expected or imagined. The glow is long gone.

"So! This is how you live, Mary Margaret Hathaway?" he snaps at me. "This is awful!"

"I'm sorry," I say, not sure what else to say. "What have I done?"

The idea that I have done something also confuses me, but for once, the guilt is not overwhelming. That confuses me more.

"Of course it's not overwhelming you, Mary. It's overwhelming *me*. Your interior life is a garbage dump."

"I don't know what you mean," I say, wanting to help him. I reach out to comfort him. He backs away with a growl.

"You're so fond of thinking," he replies, his voice breaking. "Figure it out for yourself, God damn it!"

With this, I know my Chief has gone. He doesn't swear. I do. I cannot imagine what has pushed him over the edge. Has some evil spirit taken him over? The Anasazi or some bad skinwalker come to get vengeance?

"Stop your blaming. It's your crap I'm carrying on my back. An ugly mess it is, even worse than my years in the asylum."

An asylum? Is he having a...? I let go of the thought before he hears it.

Yet what is this about his carrying my crap? I am tempted to feel ashamed, but can't. He moves around, grunting and seething, beginning to open his bundle of sacred objects. I feel it is for my next journey. But how can I trust traveling with him in this condition?

"Why are you carrying it?" I ask tentatively, so as not to set him off too far, over an edge I can't help him return from.

He stops and stares at me, narrow eyes boring into mine, then goes back to work. "I told you, we are running out of time. I can only lance so much of your boil at once as long as you're carrying it. Only if I take it on myself—a hellish task if there ever was one—can we get this job done. You'll have to lance it for me. Then, maybe—maybe!—we might have a hair's breadth of a chance of making up for the ten years we are behind."

I am prompted to use my psychic vision, what little I have. The reality of what he is saying comes into clear focus. I feel an overwhelming wave of gratitude for what he is doing. Like a boil on his back, he is truly taking on my pain, internal angst, world views and destructive tendencies. I see clearly that I am free at this moment, because he is not.

"How can I help?" I ask, feeling strong, up to the task.

He turns and sheds his cotton shirt. I gasp at a boil the size of a grapefruit on his back. It's not symbolic. It's very real. A blazing redness surrounds the thick skin, full of a greenish-yellow pus at the center. I shudder.

"Lance it," he says, handing me a hunting knife.

"I don't know how," I argue. Could he truly want this lancing to be so literal an act?

"The body is a reflection of the mind's inner world," he says in his teaching voice, but terse. "Your inner world is a sewer, a kettle of hell you keep inside. It's your job to deal with it, as it is every one's own work."

"Isn't that what we are doing?" I ask.

"Yes!" he replies, poison in his voice. "But at your pace, we will never make it. Too much, too long, too many lifetimes. I've taken on what I can, for you, but you...you!...must lance the boil. It is yours."

I look at the knife in my hand, unable to imagine cutting into Chief, or anyone. "I don't want to hurt you."

"How do you think I feel when I tell you a truth you don't want to hear? Let you see a reality you have been avoiding? We are one, Mary. What hurts you, hurts me. Now lance the God damned thing before it kills me!"

I look and see it has grown even in these few moments of conversation, now the circumference of a dinner plate and several inches high, taking up most of his middle back.

My crap, alive. Taking him over, inside and out. The boil is manifest in flesh and bodily fluid. Whatever it takes, whatever I must do, I will do. I cannot lose Chief, nor be responsible for his demise in any way.

I take the knife and hesitantly poke at the boil. The thick liquid underneath only bulges the mass out to one side, avoiding me. Chief shrieks in pain, making my heart jump and my hands shake nearly beyond control.

"Stab it!" he begs.

My jaw clenched, mercy in my heart, I gash into the boil with one great downward stroke. He screams, short and high-pitched, then falls to the ground. Turning to lie his skinny back next to the fire, he inches closer, to the edge of the pit. The knife shakes in my hand until I drop it, my free hand covering my mouth to keep the horror inside. A steady stream of pus runs out. As if seeking the fire, the ooze makes its trail into the pit, sizzling and popping like oil in the blaze.

My stomach turns, sickened to know that this filth is what I have been carrying within me. I'm drawn to see it in all its gory detail, like a passerby is drawn to a fatal traffic accident as the body bags are being filled. I gag on the putrid smell it releases.

Within me, I notice an old, maybe ancient, sadness burning away, even as the ooze boils itself in its dance with wood and flame. As the boil is drained, I feel a new emptiness created within me, new pockets of clean space. Nothin', to be sure, but a good Nothin'. A Nothin' that is fertile for something new to grow. Is this the void we seek?

"Thank you," I say to Chief.

"It is I who must thank you," he replies weakly, his voice tender again. "For carrying so much for so long. You have done it for all of us." He looks into my eyes, his own eyes sad and imploring, tired, as if this has taken too much out of him. "Thank you, too, for what you must do in the days to come. There are boils only you can wear and lance for yourself. I've done all I can."

He does not have to tell me how much this will hurt, or the rewards that await the conclusion of what must be done. I can feel it. He has shown me the way, made himself the living example, giving his own body as a sacrifice. Love, as he said, paves the way.

"Let the games begin," I whisper to the gods and goddesses of the sky, sensing that, in truth, they began long, long ago.

22

Ireland!

The drum drew me into itself quickly this time, as if eager to be of assistance. Under I went, through the tree roots, then out again, over an ocean that was flowing backward, its waves curling away from the shore. Lion appeared, explaining the odd image. We were traveling backwards through time.

Now, emerald hills roll before me. I fly against high winds over massive cliffs, hard-worked fields and miles and miles of stone walls. Celtic music plays deep in my ears.

Yes, Ireland. The land of my ancestors, though that never held enough draw to pull me to its shores, at least in this lifetime. Perhaps, though, there was another. I have to wonder, sensing that I know this place, as if I'd grown up hearing stories of leprechauns and playing with the goats that grazed in my back yard.

Lion looks at me, seeming all the more real in this journey, a true wild beast. I feel safe, yet not enough to reach down and touch her sunlight golden coat, every hair seeming as real as my own. Her power is too awesome.

Side by side, we fly as if with wings. I am amazed at how vivid everything is. The green jumps out at me as if it were an entity unto itself. The rocks seem to vibrate in tune to the curve of the hills, joining the melody I hear coming from nowhere. So, this is the living Ireland everyone raves about. Or am I seeing even more than the average tourist?

In the distance, an old stone tavern appears. I want to weep for the beauty of its simple construction, its thatched roof, its beloved place in the heart of the small community. Moving closer, I sense I am continuing to move backwards in time. The season changes to winter, the tavern now nestled in cold. Smoke curls from the chimney. A young woman approaches, wind-blown and shaking.

"Follow her," Lion instructs.

I watch and witness as a scene unfolds. Inside, there is no electricity and the dress seems very old-fashioned. "It must be two hundred years ago," I say, thinking of Scrooge.

"Yes," Lion agrees, though whether she is agreeing to the time frame or my theatrical analogy, I don't know.

The pink-cheeked woman orders a pint, then goes and rubs her hands by the peat fire. A priest is there, playing some kind of makeshift instrument and singing. I hear them speak Gaelic, but understand perfectly.

She is teasing him about finding another day to show off his string and barrel. He laughs quietly and teases her back about finding another day to come and be blessed to hear it.

"What am I supposed to be doing?" I ask Lion.

"Go close behind her," she instructs me, "to see through her eyes."

I find a place for me within her, like resting my soul upon her soul. The impact is more than I bargained for. I not only see through her eyes, I smell the stale lager and pungency of peat burning. Back in time, living through this woman, I feel a rush of emotion. Is it love?

I close my eyes to feel it, let it envelop me. Yes, love, but more. Being in love. True love. So this is what it feels like to see and be seen. My heart races with hers, my smile pure and unbroken.

Yet, who is it she loves? I answer my own question as her eyes move toward the priest. Very handsome, too handsome for his position, some say. Oh, forbidden love! Behind her eyes, I tour her memories. The charity work they have done together. Long walks on grassy fields with talks of God. The grief in his eyes when he performed the wedding her father arranged.

The priest begins to sing a ballad she knows well. A hush grows over the crowd. The bittersweet tears at my throat, burning so deeply I move back from her eyes, lift my soul away, unable to bear it. If this is love, or what comes of it, who wants it?

"You can see through the eyes of anyone," Lion says.

I move myself to the eyes of the bartender's wife. Everyone else suspects the love between these two, that he sings the ballad for her, but the bartender's wife knows. She sees it all. A seer, in fact, though she keeps her gift to herself. She's so sorry for the young woman. She knows they have never been together, and how it tears them both apart.

"A love story turned classic tragedy," I tell Lion, still wondering what the point is.

"An archetypal story," Lion agrees, "universal in nature, as most stories are. They do not see it as such, of course. For them, it is their story alone, ever immediate, ever personal. That is why we have archetypal stories, because everyone can, from some lifetime, relate. No story is unique. No role goes unplaced by each human, in one lifetime or another."

"Everyone plays all the roles?"

"There are a few divine incarnations who repeat a specific role in service to mankind," she admits, "but they are rare. Now we go on to the future."

I still feel like Scrooge, flying over time. But what is all of this to teach me?

We move away from the cold to the heat again. A summer day. In a house, at night, I see the same woman. She's pregnant, looking full term. I wonder, as I smelled the peat, if I laid my soul upon hers now, would I feel her baby's life within me? Excitement stirs, nearly leaps in me, at the thought. My only chance.

"I want to go into her again," I say. "I want to feel the baby as if it were in my belly. It may be the only time I will know what it feels like to be creating a life in my own body."

Lion dips her head to agree with my plan.

I move myself over the woman, until the strain of her belly seems to pull on my own back. Oh, my, yes! Yes, this is what I have so longed for. What I seemed to know, from a young age, would be glory.

That is, if she were not so worried. Almost frantic. The baby is due, and her husband is home. He was supposed to be away. A cramp comes, seizing us both so hard I feel the back of my jaws ache. With her, I grit my teeth. She can't pant, though she wants to. He will see.

Without warning, I feel water trickle down her legs. There is no hiding it now. The pain clamps down and she lets out a whimper.

She panics because he has seen. She asks for him to get the midwife.

He says no, getting up to come after her. Her terror enters my veins, pulsing.

"He doesn't think the baby is his!" I say to Lion.

Through her, I see her husband's dark eyes, small and ugly. My pulse soars. We can both see it coming.

"Oh, God," I hear myself say aloud, up there, hearing the drumbeat.

"Keep going, Sweet Mary," Chief speaks from the distance.

My stomach jolts me back to the scene, unfolding too realistically. The husband sends his boot flying into her belly, so that it seems to push the baby all the way up into her heart. The pain doubles me over. I am breathless.

No! He's killing the baby. Our baby. Together, we crash to the floor. Water and blood gush. I gasp for breath as the boot hits, again and again. Holy mother of God, help her. Help the baby. No infant can survive this. I'm not sure a mother can. But who cares? If the baby does not live, why would she want to?

Caught, I watch with horror as the scene unfolds about me, helpless to do anything but observe the inevitable. The baby is dead. She knows it.

"Watch closely," Lion says.

As I do, I see a layer of the mother's soul emerge. It is a faint likeness of her, like a ghost that lifts off her and goes to hover in the corner. I watch her husband spoon a liquid she knows to be poison into her mouth.

She knows he wanted it this way. He planned to do this, to wait until her longing was full-term, so he could rob her when she had the most to lose. He'll get away with it, too. His brother is the undertaker. Mothers die in childbirth all the time. No one will ever know.

She no longer cares.

I want to go back to her, to comfort her, but I am afraid. I watch from a distance as a small smile appears on her face and her eyes flutter.

"What is she thinking, Lion? Can you tell me?"

Lion moves to join with the woman to witness what I cannot bear to get close to. "She imagines her funeral. She knows her husband cannot stop her from seeing her soul mate's face one more time."

"The priest will perform the funeral?" I cry out, horrified that he must be put through it.

"Yes. Now peace is entering in. She sees the very brilliant light coming for her." I hear the peace enter Lion's voice, and wish I had waited to experience it myself.

I watch her die, while the ghost remains hovering in the corner of the room.

It all stops.

Ireland is gone. Lion is gone. I am on the dirt floor of the canyon, Chief having called me back to a double-time beat, without my even hearing it. My stomach aches. I sit up and break down, crying piteously until the tears are spent. Chief waits without motion or sound.

"What was that all about?" I finally ask, my head throbbing from the torrent of grief that has spilled.

"Lancing a boil. You did very well. This will work."

"What boil?"

Chief moves closer to me. "Did you know any of those people?"

"Know them?"

"Concentrate on the essence. As you sensed Puck's essence felt like Hannah's."

I try to match the essence of any of the characters, but to no avail. The idea of an essence reminds me again that I have made no progress in my mission. "I'm sorry, I can't make any matches. I didn't find out anything about the Essence of Ray either."

"Don't worry about that now. Remember their eyes. You can see it best in the eyes."

I attempt this, but see nothing in the handsome priest's eyes, however beautiful, that I recognize. I can't even seem to see the woman's eyes, having spent most of my time behind them.

"No," I say, sorry to disappoint Chief, who seems to be so invested in the outcome.

"What about the husband?" he asks.

I shudder, remembering again his small, cold eyes, so dark and cynical. A connection comes clear to me. "Yes! Yes, I do know who those eyes remind me of. Dark Crow!"

Chief nods sadly. "Yes, yes. Dark Crow. He has been your nemesis in so many lifetimes."

"My nemesis?" I ask, once again feeling sick to my stomach.

23

Chief did not explain further before sending me off to the waterless waterfall. Why should he have? His implication was clear enough. That I am, or was, the Irish woman from however long ago it was. A simple country woman who lived the archetypal love tragedy, then lost her child and her own life to the boot of an evil man. Dark Crow. Really, what more is there to say?

At the waterfall, the creek water had receded significantly in the short time I was away. I could only lie on the bottom of the stream, my face barely covered by the slow-moving waters. Still, I did not call on Oya for rain. Enough calling on that which is invisible.

I returned to Chief both spent and cleansed, wondering how my Irish bones had broken incorrectly, how such journeys can reset them, and where I am to go next. He assured me that there would be no more boils to lance upon my return, at least none on him.

I approach gingerly nonetheless. He sits, waiting patiently by the fire. Seeing all is well, I plunge into the one question which will not leave me be.

"How do you know your life is not a hoax?"

"Ah," he says. "The kind of hoax such as spending a lifetime thinking you are choosing not to have a child because it is a gift to God and a lost friend, when in fact the sacrifice might really be a kind of self-protection, born of fear and pain?"

"Yeah, that pretty much covers it," I reply quietly, tossing minute bits of leaves and grass into the fire, watching them burn, feeling the loss. Leave it to Chief to hit the nail on the head.

"You cannot know your life is not a hoax, Sweet Mary, because it is. You are dreaming it all. A magnificent play. You are producer, director and star. All of life is a stage."

I think of this, of Shakespeare, of the "life is illusion" theory. Of Lion's belief that we all, at one time or another, play out all the archetypes. It makes me think of all the hoaxes we conjure up. The hoax of a "Suzie Homemaker" in a three-bedroom home with a high mortgage on a cul-de-sac in the suburbs. The hoax of a fast-paced career woman with no time for a real relationship. The hoax of a woman on a spiritual quest wanting to save the world.

Chief laughs gently, kindness in his face. "You want to help save the world? You must save yourself first, because you are creating the world in the first place."

"How do I save myself?"

"Eventually, you will have to start dreaming a new dream. For now, consider all that you have learned. Not only the lost infant. There is more to the Irish life."

"The priest," I say, already knowing what he is getting at. I thought about him, too, in the creek. "If he was the Irish woman's true love, and she was me, then he was my true love."

"Yes. Though he has gone by many names, for now you can call him Ray."

"Ray?" I shout, a kaleidoscope of feelings rushing into me. "The Essence of Ray is the essence of Ray? Like a guy named Ray? I'm doing all this to find the priest from the tavern?"

"There is your own healing, too," Chief says, smiling like a man delivering a Christmas feast to an impoverished family who expected to go hungry. "But yes, you are also journeying to find the essence of Ray, so you will know what you are looking for when the time comes."

"Looking for?" I say, my heart leaping in my body. I remember Jimmy saying something about finding someone. Is it him?

"Ray need not remain only in your past. If everything goes as I am dreaming, he will also be in your future." He looks expectantly into my eyes, as if waiting for a reaction.

As high as my heart has leapt, it falls. My voice is flat, lifeless. "You won't find him. He's not here anymore."

Don't ask me how I know this, I just do. For the first time in my life I understand the huge hole in my heart. The hole that has always existed, even greater than that of being a motherless daughter. Until now, that hole never had a name. Now it does. Ray. Yet what good is finally naming something that is eternally beyond reach?

"You have lost your faith," Chief says. "Find Ray, and you will find your faith."

I nod to the truth that I have lost my faith, remembering Jimmy that said something about our not being able to live without it. I agree. Yet I know what I know on this matter. Both Ray and my faith are beyond my reach.

"You must let yourself dream again," Chief continues. "To do that, you must learn more of your lifetimes before this one. Are you strong enough to journey again?"

My stomach still aches from the last round, but I answer by moving myself into position. Chief replays his long ceremony of preparation and at last begins drumming.

Soon enough I am drifting down through the trees, under the earth, and over the ocean flowing backwards. This backward journeying takes longer than the last time. Does that mean I am going farther back in time? None of the shamans I knew told me of this sensation. Then again, symbolism did vary from shaman to shaman.

I feel a tropical breeze caress my face. Air that is warm, moist, heavily scented with a bounty of earth and foliage. Polynesia? No, Hawaii. Another place I have never been.

Lion appears below me, inviting me down. I swoop to her side, an easy landing.

"Hawaii?" I ask to be sure.

"Very long ago," Lion agrees.

Yes. There is a primitive feel to the place. Not like the tourist hot spot of today, with cars and airplanes and five-star hotels. Only people and earth. I feel the charge of the soil, steeped in volcanic action. The smell of sulfur permeates the air. I look toward the odor, and in the distance see my first active volcano. A boiling, blowing stream of red hot lava, trickling down, creating more and more island as it sizzles into the ocean. Amazing.

I feel as if I ought to be afraid, but the energy is so pure and natural, it is impossible. Everything seems to be in harmony. The palm trees reach up in celebration, as though dancing with the sky gods, while the earth holds them steady.

I would be content to gaze, but Lion moves us toward a lagoon where a bronzed native woman is dressed in grass and leaves. Her slender waist and small, firm breasts would make her a hit in any bar in the world these days. In fact, her wide lips and dark, heavily lashed eyes would have her front and center on a beauty magazine.

I don't know who this girl is, or was in my past life, but I guarantee it's not me. I've never looked half this good. Not to mention never having a composure even remotely this serene. This woman is everything I am not.

I watch her move toward the water, her hips graceful, like Kenya's, though more innocent. She is a girl in a woman's body, at one with all things. Without invitation, I float behind her eyes, lay my soul over hers.

Behind her eyes, I view her story in an instant. Born an untouchable Kauwa, she was slated alongside her fraternal twin sister to be a slave. Her shadow was never to fall upon even a Maka'ainana commoner, let alone an Ali'i of the ruling class. Yet her exquisite face saved her from the fate of her sister, who was subjected to tattoos around her forehead and eyes, the sign that told anyone and everyone "I am less than nothing—abuse me as you will."

For her beloved twin, though, she intends to change all that.

Not only beauty has saved her, but also her gift as a remarkable psychic. She understands when the rains will come, when the volcano will surge. She is one with the land and the ocean, and friend to the god, Lono. He is the one who gives her the powerful manna to carry prophecies from all the gods of the water. Soon, the messages of the gods will be given to all, that manna from the heavens is every person's birthright. Then the ruling classes will have to honor the gods by no longer abusing the Kauwas. It will all occur at the annual Makahiki celebration, which Lono resides over. Just as soon as the first sign of the Pleiades shows above the horizon at dusk.

Her intended husband, a great Kahuna, has agreed this is the time.

I feel her supple skin as she begins to remove her clothes, unashamed and innocent, yet plagued by thoughts of her people. Forced to live as prisoners in tiny enclaves, many of the men have been made a human sacrifice. She slides into the water, letting it wash away the worry, reminding herself to be grateful for her chosen role. For is she not proof that any person may have great manna?

"Who is she?" I ask Lion.

"You."

"No way. I was never this pure. Was I?"

"Move closer into her. You will know."

I do, melding my heart to hers. "Oh! Everything is so sacred in her—yes, I have to say it—*my* eyes."

Just like Chief, I once knew how to walk lightly on the earth. I knew about thanking the sand for meeting my feet, and the water for allowing me to swim. "How could I have lost this?" I ask.

"We will find out soon," Lion replies. "Why don't you take a moment to enjoy the water? I will summon you when we must move forward."

Like a child given permission to play, I dive into the deep blue water again and again, becoming the beautiful, intuitive maiden I once was. Glory, glory be! Such freedom! Such bliss! The salty water glides free over my nakedness, my stomach and leg muscles rippling as I move, my breasts unencumbered. They drink up the tantalizing moisture, feeling alive and sensual in Mother Nature's abundance. Surely, I have never been so free.

Under the water, I find another world, one of bright orange coral clumped together like overgrown bunches of cauliflower, and sunlit fish that prove, prove! the world's Creator a Master artisan. Only an artist would think of putting neon green fins, iridescent purple spines and haunting yellow stripes on something so insignificant as a fish. Just as only a Master would know there is nothing insignificant about a fish. In this Hawaiian life, I understand that.

I reach out to the fish, playing with them, telepathic to

their ways, all they know. They jump and dart, glad to see me, a friend. So this is why I have so much manna! They give it to me, freely. I remind myself to try and remember this one thing, later, when I am again up in the dry canyon as Mary Margaret. That to know what we know, we need only become one with the universe, respecting each inhabitant, even the moths and mosquitoes. They, too, have knowledge, and are willing to share it, if you are a friend. So simple. How did I forget? Why did I forget?

My own question pulls me from the water to Lion. Without speaking, she indicates we must move on. Sadly, I allow myself to be propelled forward in time. In front of me, the maiden stands at the volcano's edge, close enough to heat her beautiful face. She is dressed elaborately in orchids and other flowers. Her wedding. To Ray, I wonder? I unite with her soul again in hope.

Immediately I feel all is not well. My twin sister is frantic to get to me, yet as a slave she is barred from my wedding. "Soon, my sister," I send out the telepathic message. "Soon all of this will change."

Several bulky men guard me, keeping her away. Yet she is insistent. Something is wrong. Something I have not seen, she says without words. Our telepathy is strong. I understand she must be heard.

With authority I speak to the guards in a language I no longer know. Reluctantly, they let her in to see me.

Lion appears to my side. I had almost forgotten her. She speaks solemnly. "Look into your sister's eyes."

I do. Ray! My beloved is my sister?

"We all play many roles, experiencing all genders and many different relationships with the same souls, in one lifetime or another," Lion explains. "Do not let it distract you."

I nod, looking to my sister and soul mate. I trust her, but what she is saying now makes no sense. She is terrified, wanting to stop the ceremony. She says it's not what I think. Not a marriage, but the first woman sacrifice. She says my husband will kill me before he allows my message to be heard. It is all a trick, to get me to the volcano's edge. She believes he will call me a sorcerer and say my manna is black manna.

Looking into her beautiful eyes, I see it all. She is right. Lono has abandoned the maiden to a fiery fate. Why? Why? Her eyes widen with terror, a prisoner to the scene unfolding.

Everything moves slower. Slower still. My sister is pulled away by the hair, feet kicking and screaming. I scream for them to stop, my innocent, beautiful mouth contorted in terror. They say they won't hurt her, but they will. I can see it. I can see everything. Have always seen everything. Everything but my own demise.

Above me, where Chief drums, I feel myself reach an arm up, grasping at him, needing someone to hold onto.

"Let me come back," I say with the mouth of Mary Margaret, "I don't want to see this."

Over the distance of a thousand backward waves, I hear Chief as his drumming goes on and on. "Stay long enough to look into the eyes of your intended husband."

My stomach is a knot and my body burns from the heat of the volcano. "They're going to throw me in!"

"The eyes, Mary, see who deceives your people, holds your truth back."

Her intended husband approaches. As directed, I look into his hateful, angry eyes. Dark Crow. Again.

I watch the maiden I was as she is carried toward the spitting lava that seems eager to eat her alive. From a distance I see a part of her soul shoot up, ghostly and fragile, flying into the body of a bird. As one with the bird, she flies away. She does not look back, but the screams of her maiden-self reach her ears, and mine.

Frantic, I open my eyes and pull myself to a sitting position, only now realizing that Chief has been drumming double-time, signaling my return anyway.

"What good can possibly come of all this?" I beg to know, my feet hot, as if singed by a fire better left in my subconscious. Yet even as I ask, I understand. This process is the emotional dismemberment required of every shaman. It is an honor, assuming you make it through with your sanity intact.

24

I am losing it. Losing any sense of who I am, who I've been as Mary Margaret. Not a courageous, dedicated best friend who keeps her commitments to never having a child, but a frightened lost soul who's terrified of having, and possibly losing, another baby. Not a spiritually mature woman who has mastered her own version of floating off to be a bird in some kind of contented witnessing awareness, but a fragmented soul who uses the bird to escape what is too hard to deal with. I've always been prone to beating myself up, but those few illusions have helped me feel reasonably good about myself. Now I'm waking to a reality that bites hard. I have been a victim, over and over again. Which begs the question, why should this life be any different than the others?

If any of this is real. I've never believed in past lives. Maybe this is just my psyche's warped way of picking on what little self-esteem I have left. Maybe I'm fucked up, for sure, true and bona fide, but none of it is real, so who cares? Maybe all of us, digging deep into the darkness of our own pork and beans, would find such wacky shit.

Hell, even Chief, who I'm trusting like there is no tomorrow, admits he's spent time in an asylum. Who's to say he has his shit together enough to lead me anywhere but where he's been?

It is with these thoughts that I have made my way to the creek by the sacred waterfall, as has become the ritual. I don't know if it has any great magical powers, but I need some break in the past-life torture routine. The water seems to be evaporating as fast as my sanity. It is just past my calves now. At this remarkable rate, I give it another day before it is reduced to a stream of bubble, gurgling from the earth, struggling to remember its vast nature amid the parched realities of the canyon. Like the rest of us. I wash by scooping water up in my cupped hands, doing a half-assed job.

Ready to make my way back, I hear a small voice from a distance as it becomes clearer and clearer.

"...so I told Chief it wouldn't really be a bother," Puck says, as if I'd begun listening from a mile back, "even though you were very busy, because you liked me so very much when we met, and you knew you were The One now, and The One would want to see me, I am sure, because...."

"Hi Puck," I interrupt, now that he is only a foot from me. My heart, if it could grin, would be ear to ear.

Hannah.

"Oh, are you done already?" he asks, disappointment tugging at his voice.

"Just waiting for you," I say.

Puck strips naked, innocent of my gender, and jumps in as though it were a swimming pool full of water. He is all laughter and splash, making it useless to attempt real conversation. Yet on he goes, about one thing and then another. I laugh, tickle behind his ears, and cry waterfall tears hidden by the splashes. It is a moment, I am acutely aware, that I wish to be with me forever. As he dances in the sunlight, I bask in him, in his light, trying not to see the signs of his own torture. When at last we seem thoroughly soaked, I motion for him to join me on the sand where the sacred waterfall ought to be falling.

"...then my mother said that you can't do that, but I said you could, so I had to spend the whole day picking rocks from the yard, and now my shoulders are sore but the waterfall helps that because this is a very special waterfall, you know, only here when you really need it, I think. Did you ever think that? I think that a lot of things are like that, sometimes there only when you need them and not there when you don't or only there for some people, but other people, 'specially bad ones, can't see them, or maybe sometimes they can but hardly ever do unless they have been really good that day...."

"Puck?" I ask.

He stops short and looks at me, cocking his head and furrowing his brow, as if surprised I might have something to say. "What, Mary?"

I wonder how to start this, or if I should. Is it right to burden a child in such a way? Yet if this is Hannah, how can I not ask?

"I have a little problem. I was hoping you could give me some advice. Do you know what advice is?"

"Oh, yes," he says, his eyes lighting up. "Advice is when you tell someone what to do but they aren't going to do it. My mom gives my dad advice all the time but he doesn't do squat and she tells him that's why we are the way we are, with no money and Dad always mad at everyone. Me, I think he is only mad at himself, cause he never does what he tells himself to do, either."

If reincarnation exists, this is Hannah all right. Only five and everybody's pegged, if not downright nailed to the wall.

"Well, I'll very seriously consider doing what you suggest, if you'll tell me what you really think, in your heart."

He offers a resolved, determined face to the canyon, then returns it to me. "Okay. What is your little problem?"

I chuckle at the way he says "little problem" with such innocence, like it ought to be just that, instead of the cement block around my neck that I've been swimming with for more than two decades. "Well, a long time ago, when I was a little girl...."

Puck is listening intently, so perfectly serious I want to dispense with the whole topic and hug him till he can't stand it any more. But I want to know. I have to know.

"I made a promise to my best friend and to God. Her name was Hannah."

I hesitate, giving Puck a chance to react. He doesn't.

"Hannah died right after I made the promise, so I've kept the promise all my life. But now, I think maybe I don't need to keep it anymore, because maybe I didn't have the right reasons for making it. And nobody really cares anyway. So I was wondering, do you think someone should keep a promise like that, no matter what?"

Puck shakes his head back and forth slowly. "That's not a kid question, Mary. That's a grown-up question! I'm just a kid."

I let out my breath, not realizing I was holding it, in order to laugh whole heartedly.

I know, baby. I know. And maybe it is wrong of me to ask.

"Yeah," I continue despite my reservations, "but it was a kid promise. I think sometimes kids know a lot more than adults about those kinds of things."

"That is for sure!" Puck agrees, then thinks some more. "Do you still love your friend, even though she's dead?"

Without warning my eyes flood. I look away, blinking furiously. I even my voice as best as I can. "Yes, very much," I say. Only the last word breaks in my throat.

"Well then," he says with resolution, "even if it was wrong, I'm sure she would forgive you. You know God will, too."

I avoid the question of God, delighting in Puck's kid answer, wishing I had broken the promise along about the time his beautiful soul had been wanting to drop back into the human race.

"You do know God loves you, don't you Mary?" Puck pushes. I am noncommittal, trying to find words.

He reads my face like a kindergarten picture book. "You gotta know that, since you're The One. Don't you?"

He looks at me with wonder, as if an answer in the negative would blow his world view apart. I feel awkward, not wanting to lie, nor to burden his innocence.

"Maybe we are God, in some small way," I answer, a last-minute save that impresses even me.

He sits up straight, his face beaming, as if he's pleased to have found something to work with. "Well then, do you love yourself?"

I am stunned by the question. "I'm afraid that's an even harder one for me, Puck. But you inspire me. You really, really do."

To this my little friend smiles, puts his hand in mine and leans his head against my shoulder.

Heaven.

Slowly Puck pulls his head up, sighs and lets go of my hand. "I have to go now. My mother is looking for me."

"How do you know?" I ask.

He looks up at the sun and points, as if to indicate the time. "She forgets about me after breakfast till about now. If she remembers before I get back, she gets mad."

I wonder what will happen with him so many miles from his home. Even with his fast little feet, he will be late if she is already looking for him. Yet just as disturbing as what might happen, is what already has. How can a mother forget her young child?

"What do you mean, she forgets about you?" I probe gently.

"Well, she has problems," he says in a way that is too grown up, making me think he is repeating some adult's exact words.

"Is it very bad for you at home, Puck?" I ask, not really wanting to know, but needing for him to know that, unlike his mother, I am paying attention.

He looks away from me, appearing a bit distant and dreamy, as if he's nearly left the planet. "Sometimes, like when my dad gets really mad, then I wonder if God has problems, and he forgets about us too."

I nod with empathy, knowing the feeling, wishing I had something, anything to offer to counter the evidence. Wishing I could explain that this is exactly why knowing God loves me is a hurdle that, most days, is posted higher than I can jump.

"Now that I have met you and Chief, though, I think God has remembered us again."

Oh, the magic of this child! "I think that is the nicest thing anyone has ever said to me."

I get down on one knee to look him in the eye. "I wish I could tell you so many things, about who you are, and why things are the way they are. But I'm only learning myself. I can't really help you yet, because I don't know how. Can you understand that?"

He nods, though I see in his eyes he does not understand. How can an adult be so lost, and what does it mean that The One come to help doesn't know anything either? I can only offer him what Kenya offered me.

"I met a woman," I explain. "Her name is Kenya, and she knows everything that has ever happened in the whole wide world."

His eyes are wide in absolute belief.

"She said she knows all about you and what you want. And

all about angels, and how to help us. She says that if we keep dreaming about what we really want, it has to happen. It's like a law of God. I know for a fact she has heard you dreaming, and she knows you love the angels. So keep dreaming and talking to them about your dreams. Promise me, Puck. Promise me you'll keep dreaming your biggest, brightest, best-ever dreams."

"I promise," he says, his tone steeped in the purity of a child's conviction.

"Okay," I reply, "and I will dream, too. I'll dream of God remembering us all, especially you. Because you, young man, are worth remembering."

He looks at me like he's fallen in love.

"Now go, so you don't get in trouble."

"Okay," he says, giving me a hug and darting off.

A moment later, I hear him, his words fading as he goes. "I'm dreaming, Mary. I'm dreaming!"

25

While Puck dreams, I journey again.

Chief's drum, my seducer, beats on. My mind resists but cannot keep up. I feel myself succumbing. Lion appears. My fear disappears. We travel over the backwards ocean, farther and farther, farther still. The traveling feels slower this time. Why?

In answer, a young man, sixteen or seventeen, appears to my left. With pure skin, high cheekbones and ruby lips, he is more beautiful than any woman I've seen. He begins to travel with me, over the waves.

"Balinas of Cappadocia," he says by way of introduction.

I look at him blankly.

"An incarnation of Proteus," he explains. "You would know Cappadocia as Turkey today."

"Oh," I say, still in the dark.

"Proteus?" he prods my remembrance. "The shapeshifting God of the Greeks? Student of Hermes?"

"Oh, right," I say. Greek gods, in my journey?

"Alchemy," the boy says, now sounding exasperated.

That word I know. "Turning base metals into gold, right?"

Balinas bows in earnest. "We alchemists believe that the same methods used to turn base metals into noble metals can be used to raise that which is base within man himself into that which is noble. A painful, difficult process of seven stages—calcination, dissolution, separation, conjunction, fermentation, distillation, and finally, coagulation."

"Okay," I say, only half-able to apply my understanding of these words to any kind of personal process. What is this guy doing in my journey?

"In the first stage," Balinas continues as we slowly fly, "that of calcination, there is the burning off of the personality to reveal one's soul. In the end, with coagulation, comes a mobile state of consciousness, the Philosopher's Stone, which creates in a person a presence that can transform the reality of everything around him. Or her."

"And this has what to do with me?" I ask, not really believing it has a thing to do with me. I've just stumbled upon some lost god looking for someone to lecture to as we travel between worlds.

He responds with huge authority in his voice, as though he is quoting the word of God directly. "Separate the Earth from Fire, the Subtle from the Gross, Gently and with Great Ingenuity. It rises from Earth to Heaven and descends again to Earth, thereby Combining it Within Itself the Powers of both the Above and Below."

He stares at me like I am supposed to get it. Then, suddenly, I do. Like dominos falling, it all clicks. I remember the meaning of the entire Emerald Tablet, the one piece of writing that reveals the miracle of alchemy. I've done this before, I realize. In yet another lifetime. I was a young man, nearly as earnest as this one. Eons ago, I studied day and night, both the science and the personal transformation. I only got so far in my training, but knew one day I would come back to it. Is that what this is about?

"What now?" I ask with a tone of voice that finally offers reverence to this great Master.

"Separate the Earth from Fire," he repeats, "the Subtle from the Gross, Gently and with Great Ingenuity."

I smile. He smiles, knowing I get it.

"Time to split," he says, more like a teenager of this day and age than a god, and then is gone.

As if taking his lessons with him, my deep remembering of the alchemical process fades, like a light on a dimmer switch, until all is dark. Only his last words echo in my brain. "Time to split."

Whatever.

Again I soar across the backward flowing water, hearing Chief's drum as the waves roll toward the ocean in ever increasing speed.

"Where to this time?" I ask Lion.

"China. Early twelve hundreds," she replies.

Another place I have not traveled as Mary Margaret. Why is this? Have I avoided these places, without realizing why, because each holds broken bones? I had thought I avoided China as a protest to their torturous treatment of the Tibetans. Was it more than that?

Lion alerts me to survey the land below us. I feel a severe tightening of my gut. Already I don't like this place. Whatever happened here, I don't want to know. One thing is for sure. I'm not melding souls with anyone.

"Just watching from behind their eyes will be sufficient," Lion says, "for now."

Below us appears a town. Hangchow, I seem to know. Lion points to a boy below—a chubby, restless, snotty-nosed rich kid. Living in a grand house, one I sense is owned by a family of imperial decree. It is deeply familiar to me. The bamboo structure resting on sandalwood pillars, each spaced some three yards apart. The glazed tile roof of bright yellow and jade. The slightly upturned roof edges that make the house look like it is smiling, hosting dozens of terra cotta ornaments, from dragons to phoenixes. Even as a child, I always believed dragons were protectors instead of monsters. Could this have something to do with that?

I ought not have this horrible feeling churning up my stomach. Everything is, by the looks of it, quite lovely. A house situated in perfect harmony with the landscape, blending in with each tree and curve of hill. Decorative, oil-painted paper windows to greet you from a distance. Yet in these journeys, harmony has a way of falling apart at the first sign of trouble, like paper windows in a storm. My stomach churns on.

Lion suggests I swoop down to see behind the boy's eyes as he plays with a huge array of elegantly carved toys. Reluctantly, I do. He's not totally rotten. There seems to be some heart, deep inside. But he is spoiled, and he lords his family's position in a wimpy kind of way, so that he is strongly disliked by other children. He pretends it doesn't matter, but I sense it does. Dark Crow? Could this be where it all started for him? I'm not ready to look into his eyes.

"That is all you need to see for now," Lion suggests. "Move forward in time."

Bracing myself, I move what feels to be many years forward. A stench worse than the sulfur of the volcano rises to overtake me, even before I am looking through anyone else's eyes. Death and bodily decay, infected wounds, urine and feces all assault my senses, knocking me backwards, though there is nowhere to go. My nostrils revolt shut, so I must breathe through my mouth as my stomach contorts into dizzying somersaults.

We approach some kind of jail at the edge of a swampy field. I try to tell myself it is just a movie of the mind, but even up there, in the reality of Mary Margaret, I don't go to movies like this.

Inside the jail, a guard appears, the rich kid now grown.

"Can we hurry this up?" I ask Lion.

"See behind his eyes," she replies.

I do, though I am careful to keep my soul at a safe distance from his. He has lost his social position, been kicked out of his royal home. His father accused of embezzlement, the guard now has this lowly position, though he is the one in charge. No longer fat, he's weak, pathetic. All grown up, and angry. Dark Crow. Has to be.

The guard's only delight in life is a foreign prisoner. A man. The prisoner sings each night, soft and low, offering songs that move the guard in ways he does not want to examine too closely.

"Closet gay, to be sure," I say to Lion. "He doesn't want to admit it to himself, let alone anyone else." I know the energy, having been raised by just such a man. Is it him?

"Focus on the here and now," Lion instructs.

By the guard's orders, the foreigner is not to be tortured by anyone but him. In this way, he protects the prisoner's life. All the others come and go in weeks. But the guard makes sure he gets this prisoner a little more food, and treatment that, while still brutal, does not endanger his life.

"It's like he owns him, like a pet," I say. "Pathetic. This is the reason I won't buy anything made in China today. Because they still do this, they torture and kill."

I want Lion to be proud of me for my political activism and high standards, but she appears indifferent, as if I am missing something altogether.

I press on, wanting to vomit from the guard's sickening thoughts of sexual satisfaction with a nearly starving man half-covered in open flesh wounds. I wonder, shuddering at the thought, if the prisoner is me. Whatever the case, I want to get on with it.

"This is all very interesting," I say sarcastically, "but why do I need to see it?"

Lion looks at me with sad eyes. "Look into their eyes."

Reluctantly, I pull away from the guard to look at his eyes directly, then the prisoner's.

"No!" I scream, in here and up there, so loud I hear myself drown out the drum.

26

In the eyes of the foreigner I see what I cannot bear to see. Not me, but Ray. He is the prisoner, the one with the courage.

Worse, Dark Crow is not the guard. I am.

"I don't believe it," I say to Lion, even as I feel the bones breaking.

"Watch," Lion insists. At least she has not asked me to lay my soul upon the guard's.

The scene plays out, surreal and lifelike at the same time. I cannot mold my soul to this ugly, small guard's. I cannot believe it is me. Or ever was. This is some mistake, some detour. Some glitch in my warped psyche. I watch, convincing myself as I go. He can't be me. I don't even kill spiders. Torture my beloved? Not a chance.

We move forward without my permission, everything taking on a life of its own. My stomach churns from deep inside as the night serenade begins. The other guards have been sent out. In the distance, music plays, loud and bawdy. Women for hire have come for the other guards, and already things have turned sexual. It stirs the loins of the guard.

Yet the prisoner is unaware, singing in a weak but sincere voice. The guard's desire to possess this man is evident. He approaches and the prisoner moves away, surprised. The guard moves again, lifting his spiked baton in threat.

"There's no way this is me," I say to Lion, sure of my self.

"We are all light and dark," she replies.

I watch the threatening seduction, the prisoner pulled to hands and knees, his thread-bare clothes ripped away, exposing him.

"This is sick!"

Lion says nothing.

The guard reaches to feel his sunken belly and ribs sticking out. The prisoner whimpers as the guard releases himself from his own pants.

Yet he is unable to do it. Limp.

"He can't!" I say excitedly. "It's because he loves him too much to take him in such a horrible way."

The guard reaches out to touch the matted hair of the prisoner, who is silently weeping.

They stay together for what seems forever, until a subordinate comes into the jail. The guard quickly moves away, feeling sick and ashamed. The subordinate asks what is going on.

I cannot believe what I am seeing. The guard hands his spiked baton to the subordinate.

"But it will be the prisoner's death sentence!" I cry out to Lion.

"Look into the subordinate's eyes," she suggests.

Dark Crow. The two guards exchange a knowing look. Dark Crow is to do his dirty work. With a curt nod, the deal is struck.

I see a ghostly form of a soul rise up out of the guard that is supposed to be me. The form moves away, unable to bear his own agreement.

"No," I say, not to Lion, but to Chief.

I have not waited for his drum to beat at double-time to open my eyes and sit up. This is too much.

Chief does not stop me. It is as though he knows it has all gone too far.

I'm out of here. This is insanity. I want no part of it. Maybe my life as a researcher is small, and has no great meaning, but this kind of life will make me disappear altogether.

Ignoring me, Chief continues drumming. I understand. He is letting me decide, letting me make my own choice.

I'll miss him. An understatement. I swallow against a brick in my throat.

Standing, I get my land legs and gather my things to the incessant beat of the drum. I wonder, like the Telltale Heart, will I hear it even after I am gone, until it drives me insane?

I gather my water and look to the sky. Mid-afternoon on who knows what day it is. In the Lion's Mouth, I can't remember. I figure I can make it to Spider Rock in a few hours, out of the canyon by nightfall. Call Eric, take a hot bath at Thunderbird Lodge, and be gone.

Just be gone.

If Chief is listening in on my thoughts, he leaves me with them. I guess that is one proof of who he is; that he lets me go without protest. A lesser man would argue, try to convince. Tears line the rims of my eyes, making it hard to see what I am doing. I can blink them back. But I cannot blink back the truth that, however badly this has turned out, I have had the privilege to know a great, great man. That will never be changed by the fact that I could not walk the path he set forth.

There is not much to take, my purse and bags, my two water bottles—just what I came with. I want to touch Chief to say good-bye, but even the smallest gesture, the lightest touch of my fingertips on his arm, would shatter me into a thousand pieces.

"Good-bye," I say mentally, certain he can hear me. Also certain I am leaving the most beautiful human that I've known, perhaps that the world has ever known.

This lingering will do no good.

There is lead in my feet, but I take each step with conviction. I simply cannot be a part of Chief's plan, whatever it was. Either that guard was me, and I am wholly unworthy, or he wasn't me, and I'm one screwed-up puppy. Either way, my time is up. Someone else will have to choose herself for this trip. Some woman with more courage than I have, even with the Holy People laying out my path and a lion at my side.

I half want to pray the Anasazi or some wild animal gets me, but that feels like a death wish. My Catholic fear of suicide, so deeply instilled in childhood, does not allow me such wishes. I'm stuck, again, in Nothin'.

Clouds provide a shade, as if to ease my journey back, when I would prefer a bearish beating, even lightening to crack at me from every which direction. I cannot find it in myself to become the bird. Maybe I never will again. The thought saddens me, but still the tears won't leap beyond the rim.

My pace feels painstakingly slow. I find a glimpse of redemption through the suffering. I have never understood the lure of self-mutilation, until now. What pleasure it would be to have physical pain to distract me from the emotions that sear and slice at the heart.

The walk is long, a dull agony of great magnitude in which I cannot help but revisit those China days. Though it was not me, simply won't compute as me, perhaps it was. If so, I'm no one to be saving any part of the world. I suppose I have always known there were demons inside of me, evil strong enough to destroy the very ones I love. Like Hannah. If I was The One, I'd have seen it in advance and saved her. But I didn't. A seer who didn't see the most important event in her life coming. Hell, even today I can see Puck's pain, yet am unable to help.

I allow myself the fantasy of finding him, taking him with me. But I am split now, as Balinas predicted, nearly insane. I can feel it, only half of me here, all the rest of my soul in bits and pieces, out there in different spaces and times. How could such a soul save anyone?

Besides, what if I beat Puck too? What if that is the reason behind the reason behind the reason I chose not to have a child? Because I am a danger to him, and I have always known it?

Absurd.

Right. It is absurd. I would not hurt that little boy even the least bit before I would cut off my own hands. So how could it be I would harm Ray? My true love? Or anyone?

No, it's not true. Doesn't make sense. I know who I am. Who I am not. I do not harm those I love. I do not.

Slow mile upon slow mile passes until at last I see ahead of me the curve that leads to Spider Rock. Beyond that, civilization, Navajo style. Back into the land of the living. Then at the Thunderbird Lodge, sanity again. Unless it has all blown up. At this point, anything is possible.

I walk around the bend just as the sun comes out, half expecting to run into a load of Nelson's passengers. Indeed, the heap of soldered steel is there. No passengers, though. Only our friendly tour guide, sitting on a folding lawn chair, his feet propped up on the edge of a tire, his cowboy hat sitting more on his face than head. He tilts it to me as I approach—a solemn, understanding gesture—but says nothing. I walk right past him.

A few heartbeats later I hear him behind me, trying to catch up. I don't slow.

"Hold up," he says, hurrying his barrel-chested frame.

I stop to look at him. "So," I say, bitterness lacing each syllable, "did you know the appointed time of my failure, or have you had to wait?"

"Figured you'd make it at least a day," he says, not joking. "Been waiting since then."

I offer a glare I would not want to face. "Why did you bring me here, if you knew I would not make it? If you knew I would fail Chief and everyone else?"

He holds his hat in his hands, like the gentleman he is, looking nervous. Like he has a job here, and it is important, but he has no idea how to go about it.

"Anyone in their right mind would question what's going on," he says.

"You're right about that," I say, turning again to walk.

He keeps up, this time without missing a beat. "Sometimes you gotta lose your mind, though, to find your heart."

"Sounds very movie-of-the-week," I retort, knowing I'm not being fair. But then, life isn't fair. Haven't I learned that one well enough?

"Don't you want a ride?" he asks.

"Not at the price of you trying to talk me into going back."

"I just got one story to tell you, that's all. Just let me tell it and you can do whatever you want from there."

I sigh, too weak and weary to keep up the fight in any steady manner. "I know about the Navajo teaching stories. But I'm all taught out. I just want to get out of here."

"You come this far, don't you want to know why? Who you are?"

"Who everyone thinks I am, you mean? No, I don't need to know that. Salt in the wound."

"Well, then, do it for me," he says, sounding forlorn, lost.

I shake off the ploy, needing to stay on my toes.

"What's in it for you?"

"I've got a mission, too. May not seem like much to someone like you, someone of your great purpose, but I'm The One for mine."

"And that is...?"

"To bring you here and tell you a story. Your story."

"Who told you this story? Chief? He could have told me himself."

"A lion told me," he says, deadpan.

He has my attention, but I'm not easily swayed.

"You want me to listen to a story a *lion* told you?" I ask, heartless in my mocking. God, there's good reason to hate myself.

He startles me by opening his button down rodeo shirt. Across his huge chest is a stripe of scars from above the left nipple to just below the navel, a slashing that has produced an elegant yet ghastly deep curve. It will mark him for life. The stripes are closed, yet still swollen and red, indicating the wound is a few weeks old, at the most. I stare, knowing that this, like Chief's boil, is a reality that cannot be denied.

"Yes," he says, "I want you to listen to a story a lion told me."

The wound begs both admiration and sympathy. Even I'm not that heartless. If he took a real honest-to-God lion's lashing for a story that has anything even remotely to do with me, I'll just have to listen. Not believe it, of course, nor let it sway me. I'll just hear him out, to be polite, and be gone. I'd have given that much to the African shaman with a sliced-off heel.

I nod, turning back to the jeep. "Get me out of the canyon before you say a word. And button your shirt. You don't want to be uncovered in the sun." Truth is, I don't want to see it. I've got some swollen scars of my own right now.

We get into the jeep and drive, leaving Spider Rock in all her majesty, not to mention Chief and any hope I had of changing the world, behind me for good.

I muse that maybe this is how it always is and always will be. That man will fail, the Anasazi and the U.S. Military and the Mary Margaret Hathaways of this tiny speck of time on Mother Earth will fuck up everything, again and again, yet the Spider Rocks will endure. I like the idea.

My guide drives without speaking—a man of his word— but I can feel the wheels turning in his head. He's trying to plan out how he's going to tell me what I don't want to know. My own wheels turn, at half speed only, considering how I'm going to hear the story without it pushing me over the edge.

The drive goes on forever it seems. At last we exit the canyon, make our way onto the main road and finally pull over a few miles past the scenic overlook at Spider Rock. Nelson points to a ledge a half mile from the road, saying something about not being disturbed. I do not respond, only cross the hard rock, jumping cracks and steadying myself in its little hills and valleys. At the rim we settle in, our legs dangling dangerously over the side, as if it were a ten-foot ledge instead of the massive drop it is.

Another wave of vertigo overtakes me. This time it comes like an invitation, even a reasonable excuse. I feel a huge urge to simply tilt myself forward until the momentum becomes too much. Let Mother have her child, dust to dust. My eyes roll back into my head, seducing me into oblivion.

"Not yet, Mary," Nelson implores, giving my shoulder just a touch. "Not until you know who you really are."

27

"This story is about the beginning of time," Nelson begins, his voice low and slow, sounding thickly Navajo, even more so than usual. It is as if he feels the sacredness of his task takes him straight to his roots and it oozes out his dialect.

"Is this a Navajo legend?" I interrupt, wanting a box to put it in so I can write it off. There are plenty of creation legends, after all, and I am not Navajo. At least not in this lifetime. These don't have to be my answers, just because I am here, and my storyteller is sounding baritone and sure, like God Himself.

"No," he says, surprising me, "not according to Lion. She told me there are many creation stories, almost as many as people, even though most people follow someone else's story. Each person's story is true for the one who lives it. This story here is your story. Your beginning."

"Makes sense," I say, giving in a little. Why make it harder than it has to be?

"In the beginning, there was God," he says.

I want to say I know this story, that we all know this story. But he's in his element, his eyes steady, deep in concentration, so I hold my tongue. Besides, if this was a Navajo story, he wouldn't use the term God. So, "God" help me, I'm intrigued.

"God was all there was, no world, no universe, no galaxies. God only, the Great Spirit, the Great Energy. This Great God could do anything God wanted. But God had nothing to do."

"Bored?" I interject.

He shrugs. "God decided to make something. The only materials God had to work with, though, was God."

He looks out over the distance into the open canyon before us. I nod for him to go on, captivated despite myself. Must be the passion he brings to his task.

"God started working up a storm out of God's self, working up a sweat, sweating God out of God."

"Sweating?" I challenge. Then again, if this is my creation story, being born of the sweat of God seems appropriate.

"I got to stop the story here to tell you something about stories, at least when they come to be about God. A story can't come close to what really is. Like a winter in the canyon here, so bitter cold you can forget your name if you stay out too long. You can use lots of other words to describe it. But until you been through one season, until you've forgotten your own name for hours and sometimes days, you aren't never going to come close, you know?"

"I understand. So God didn't really sweat, it's just a metaphor."

"Yeah. But don't let the story go, because it's not even close. Go into it, so you can get closer."

"Good point," I say, thinking this guy is not only a healer, he is wise. Maybe a lion's slashing does that to you. Or life out here, in the rock. I try to imagine an all-powerful entity sweating. It's easier than I expect, so long as you don't ask me to buy it hook, line and sinker.

"And don't forget what Chief says about stories."

"I know, they are only stories. I did listen to him, you know."

He smiles as if satisfied enough to continue. "Just like a person sweats from every part of his body, God sweat from every bit of God, drops and more drops of God. Different drops, depending on what part of God they came from. Then, like the generations, from every drop of God another, less potent God was born. From those Gods, more Gods, and on and on."

I imagine it in my mind, a universe of God drops.

"Every drop is beautiful. Every drop is different. The first drops, they are the most powerful. They have the most essence of God in them. They are the First Creators, the First Light, the First Emotion. Very powerful."

"Yes," I say, careful not to get sucked in.

Come on, ease up, girl. It's only a story.

"Now," Nelson says, "imagine that each drop creates its

own galaxy, and its own way of being, and every one is different, but they are all powerful."

I like the way Nelson says powerful, like a cannon shot out at first light.

"Drops of God make Drops of God," he says, his voice growing in majesty, "make Drops of God, a hundred times, a thousand times, and even further down the line, till you can't imagine how far down the line it has gone. Even these drops, way down the line, are full of power, able to create universes, and within them, worlds, like this one."

He looks at me to see if I'm following. I nod eagerly, despite myself.

"So one of these drops, a mere hint of the essence of God, created this universe, and inside it, this earth. Another drop added all the life forms. Another drop its laws of nature—like the law of opposites, making every high have a low, every light a dark, every good an evil. 'Cause you know, now that God is made manifest, he's got a front and a back. Can't have a front without a back."

I nod once to show him I'm with him, now feeling like this is not so new a story to me at all. I've heard these philosophies before, in countless ways. I suppose that does not make them true or untrue, just not new. About all that is new, so far, is the idea of the drops which, while charming, is hardly going to make it into the pages of *Physics World Today*. I give myself a mental high-five for staying in reality.

"So the Essential Drop that was Creator to this world, your world, set a big pendulum in motion, black and white, and everything in between, all set into motion with a big swoosh." He uses a grand hand gesture, from his heart out into the canyon, to emphasize his point. "It naturally had to swing too far in both directions again and again before it could come to any point of balance."

He looks at me. "You have seen the extremes of good and evil."

"Yes," I reply.

He breathes deeply and plunges in again. "It was known that the pendulum could swing so far as to destroy the earth. That has happened more than once already."

I nod, remembering that science has proven the earth has had distinct eras of life, and the Navajo also believe that this is the fifth world.

"Then Lion told me we are at an extreme of one of those swings again. She said the living creatures may not survive, but it's no big deal if it goes too far again."

"No big deal?" I ask.

Then he leans toward me and says softly, "I gotta tell you, I had a hard time with that part myself."

I nod. "Continue."

"Lion said God cannot be destroyed, not any part of God. So if the pendulum swings too far and the planet dies, then all the God that is here will simply take another form somewhere else. The soul of the place will go on, as we do, lifetime after lifetime."

"That's a pretty callous outlook," I protest.

"So thought Norbu, one of the more essential drops of God."

"Norbu?" I ask, shuddering from head to tailbone. I had heard the name in Tibet many times, given how common it is. Every time I had this same reaction. Like Truth with a capital T had come calling, only I could not find the door. When I asked what it meant, I was told "wish-fulfilling jewel." That explained my sense that I could not find the door. The only things I wished for seemed way out of reach.

He smiles widely, knowing he's got me, getting up to tell the story with more gusto. "Norbu loved this earth. Loved the concept, and the beauty, even loved the people, for all their pendulum swings. A great drop, that Norbu."

"Who is this Norbu?" I ask, feeling excitement, like we are finally on to something that could matter.

He shrugs. "Just another drop of God."

"But an essential one," I seek to confirm.

"You might say one of the higher ups. Because Norbu does not want to see the earth destroyed, Norbu decides to help. Decides this outside of time and space, which are not real things anyway. So Norbu makes a plan. To become human and help."

"Like a bodhisattva," I add eagerly, hoping he knows the term.

"Like a bodhisattva of bodhisattvas."

"Now that's power," I comment.

"The power of love," he adds. "But there was a problem. Norbu was so powerful, Norbu couldn't incarnate as a human. Couldn't get heavy enough to stay on the earth."

I get the image of trying to catch lightning in a bottle. "So?"

"Norbu does what drops of God have always done. Norbu splits in two."

He looks at me like he has a punch line coming. I offer an eager expression, egging him on.

"But then Norbu was still too much! Too grand for the human condition. So one half split again. Norbu is now three. One, too strong to incarnate without being seen for the God Norbu is. The two others that, while great souls, were diluted enough to be able to undertake the lessons of life just as other humans do. Because how could Norbu help, if Norbu was not willing to understand from direct experience? How could Norbu bring healing to pain that Norbu had never felt?"

"This is really interesting," I say impatiently, "but how is this *my* story?"

"Hold on. You have to hear it all or you won't understand."

"Okay," I say, sitting on my hands to help contain myself.

He sits again, closer to me, speaking with all the more reverence.

"The two that could incarnate were still very powerful essences of God. Split, they were the essence of Faith and the essence of Hope. Now, Faith and Hope are always the forerunners of Love. So the great one, the Norbu at half power, was the essence of Love."

"And the greatest of these is love," I say, beginning to see where at least this story leads into yet another. I remember Jesus spoke of faith, hope and love.

"You're not talking Jesus, are you?"

"Lion said you would ask that. She said Jesus was another Divine Essence, but a different one. An Essence that served his time. Like Buddha and Mohammed served in their times. Now, as the pendulum reaches its height, with technological power and a new level of consciousness awakening, it is Norbu's time."

"Wow," I say, suddenly feeling the urge to walk, to pace actually. I get up, half expecting Nelson to stop me, given the proximity to the edge. He doesn't.

"And Norbu is going to save the world?"

"The world is one of free will, but Norbu has so much love, and so much power to dream a new dream, that Norbu has agreed to bring the message of how to do it. It is not an accident that the time is now, when the pendulum swing is so close to the edge of earth annihilation."

"How do we do it, then?" I ask, walking dangerously near the edge of the canyon cliff side. I don't care. This story is far more dangerous to me than the cliff. I can feel it. Even vertigo can't pull me from this lesson. It feels written in the sands of time.

"I don't know," he says matter of factly, looking at me like I should know, like he is asking me.

"Well, I sure don't know," I say, absolving myself of that burden without a further thought. "Hell, I brutally beat and have my mortal enemy kill the ones I love the most. Don't expect any great understanding out of the likes of me."

"I know you don't know. We are, in fact, waiting for the messenger, The Divine Incarnation of Love as seen through the essence of Norbu. Lion says the messenger is late."

My nervousness has affected my whole body. I'm shaking, that capitalized Truth having gripped me by the neck. Didn't Chief say we're ten years late?

"Right, but what this has to do with *me*? I mean I know they think I am The One, but we both know I am not the Divine Incarnation of Love."

"No, you are not," he says. I breathe the biggest sigh of relief of my life, maybe the biggest ever in human history.

"You are," he continues in words that explode in my skull, "the Divine Incarnation of Hope as experienced by the essence called Norbu. You are here in this epoch of human history to be the Holy Mother of the Divine Incarnation of Love."

28

There are some things about which you don't have to tell yourself to know what you know. You just do. It's in your bones, deep in the genetic memory of every cell of your marrow. Two things I know like this. First, I am who Nelson says I am. Second, the Universe is in deep shit if it is depending on me to be the mother of anything.

"You must be insane!" I scream, not at Nelson, but into the vast canyon, the Lion's Mouth I thought I had escaped. I feel I am addressing God, or at least the biggest drop of God I can fathom. My words echo back again and again, as if mocking me.

I turn for Nelson's response. There is little, only a calm waiting as he rolls a piece of tumbleweed between his fingers, plucked out of the cracks of earth ledge. Ah, the simplicity, the luxury a tumbleweed life affords! Yet even this tumbleweed had the unlikely destiny of being picked to serve a purpose beyond what any ordinary tumbleweed might expect. Here, today, of all places, it happens. A man chooses to play with it, give it a purpose, however casual. The tumbleweed could hardly have imagined being any such toy, until this man decided to pick it, for his own amusement, his own folly.

"Is that all we are?" I ask, this time addressing Nelson, my voice slicing the eerie evening silence. A dark blue sky has become streaked with the pinks of evening, ignoring the suffering of humanity with its easy, distant beauty. "Are we God's toy? God's idea of playing marbles with universes? God playing with God's very fucking fine own self!?"

Nelson does not answer. I can hardly blame him. I would not want to contend with me right now either. I turn again to the canyon, my true nemesis, greater than Dark Crow on his worst day. "What about the suffering?" I scream. I throw my arms open to indicate all that is in my vision. "Your dream is a fucking *nightmare*...."

It all just echoes back.

My storyteller remains silent, letting me get on with my tantrum, an urgent frustration that is lifetimes old. The echo dies out, the sun sets another inch, and I am face-to-face with a reality I've long searched and even begged for.

I whirl to face him. "Where is Faith, anyway? The other third?"

I know and remember all at once. Ray. My soul mate, who is more my essential twin than I could have imagined. The one I know is gone, beyond this earth, beyond my hope.

"Am I to do this alone?" This thought leads me to further absurdity. "Oh hell, I hope another virgin birth isn't expected, because I've blown that one for sure."

I turn to yell again into the canyon. "You'd think the Big Drop would have noticed that by now."

"Lion did not speak of those details," he says softly. "But the last virgin birth pretty much screwed up sex for everyone in the last two thousand years, so it might be a good idea to have a regular woman give us the next Great Messenger. Even if she is a white woman."

"Yeah," I say, trying to shift to my thinking brain, bail me out of my own emotions. How do you get out of something like this? Something you know, however crazy, is true? An idea comes, like a gift. Make him prove it.

"You know, all this is a little much to take in. I'm gonna need some proof. Did Lion offer any of that? Something to get me beyond all these head games? Because if the God who knows me, Mary Margaret, is behind this, then this God knows I'm a show-me-the-money woman."

"What kind of proof do you want?" he asks without fanfare, as if he's just a waiter taking my order.

I have to think. What would do it? What could make me turn around and go back in there, back to Chief, to the drumming that still resounds in the back of my head?

Ah! I have it!

"A miracle. Not performed by you, or Chief, or even a real lion. No, no. I want to perform a miracle. My own. If I'm any kind of Divinity, I ought to be able to pull off a miracle."

"I think you're gonna have to talk to Chief about that," he says, smiling like he knows something I don't know.

"Why are you smiling?" I demand.

"It's just that getting back to Chief's gonna be a miracle."

"Why? What's happened to him?" The thought of losing Chief, for any reason, sends a panic to my heart. It was one thing me leaving him, with the chance to return if I chose. It is another thing entirely for him to abandon me and this mission.

"He's okay. But you're in for a kind of shock."

"Why?" I look at him with raised eyebrows, hands on my hips.

"Because you're already performing a miracle. You just don't know it yet."

I try to get at what he's getting at, and can't. My brain is working on half-power at best. I drop my hands. "You know, it's been a hell of a long day, so just tell me."

"Getting back to Chief is going to be a miracle because you're already there."

I look away, then back at him. "What does that mean? I'm dreaming this?"

I lunge at him, grab his arm. "Feel this. Flesh and blood. You are not a dream." I put his other hand on my other arm and flex. "I'm not a dream, either. This body is right here, right now."

It is all he can do to keep from laughing. "I never said you were not here. I only said you were down there, with Chief in the canyon, too."

"No. I walked half way out of that canyon and you drove me the rest of the way." Even as I say this, I realize that I don't feel all here. It scares me.

"You are right. At the same time, you stayed there. Divine Incarnations can do that."

I don't respond, because I can't.

"You knew you had to leave," he continues, "because you could not take it any more. You also knew you had to stay, because you couldn't imagine abandoning Chief when you'd finally found him. So you did both. By most people's account, a miracle."

"That is ridiculous," I stutter.

"See for yourself."

"How?" I ask, not believing a single word. Not a half a word of what he is saying. Saint Francis of Assisi, maybe. Chief, okay. Me, no way in hell.

He grows quiet and his face becomes serious again. "You do it by choosing to."

I don't know what to say, so I look to him for help, hanging on a limb of reality that is damn near ready to snap.

"This is where it all comes down to it," he continues. "Your whole existence comes right down to this exact minute." He presses his pointer finger down into the earth, squashing what is left of the tumble weed, for emphasis.

"To become what you are, you have had to come to what you are not. Hope has to lose all hope, and choose hope again, when there's none to be found. The ultimate act of creation, born in the void. The ultimate decision of what you are going to create. All your lifetimes up to this moment have brought you to the hopelessness that split you into two."

"Time to split," I whisper, remembering Balinas.

"Now you gotta decide which of the two of you is real. Mary, the bookmobile driver, who I'm gonna take back to Window Rock. Or Mary, the Divine Incarnation of Hope as expressed through the essence of Norbu. Still in the canyon."

"Then what?" I ask, not wanting to decide. Not yet.

"Kinda simple. Once you decide, the other you will sort of fade away into what was possible, but not chosen."

Like Chief at our first meeting. Didn't he say he let go of the second version of himself before turning into the dog again?

"But which me is really real?" I ask, not so much confused anymore, as wanting time to think, to make a choice that challenges everything I've ever believed.

"Whichever one you choose," he replies. No doubt he knows he's not supposed to help me, that this must come from me, and only me.

Which one? The Mary that stays and sees this through, or the Mary that chalks it all up to impossible, returns to a bookmobile convincing herself that it was all a crazy dream—

forever saying that someone ought to be saving the world and it's too bad I don't know how or was not brave enough to try.

"I don't know," I say to myself and the canyon. I don't even know who to turn to for help.

Nelson shifts to squat on his knees. "Wyunetta Morningstar was in my clan. She used to tell me stories when I was little. Can you stand one more?"

Wisdom from my Great Mother, meeting me here, now, in my hour of need?

"Please," I reply humbly.

"Wyunetta was always an interesting woman. She had a lot of crazy ideas of her own. But she got really wild when her baby girl died. She was too angry for even the shamans to help, so she set out to talk to Black Jet Woman about it all."

"Black Jet Woman?" I ask.

"Yes. She is the winter aspect of the great goddess you would call 'Changing Woman.' She sits on her haunches and hides herself in the dark. Wyunetta used to go off at night looking for her, demanding answers to her many questions."

Like mother, like daughter. Ever shooting the moon, be it with dark cards or dark goddesses.

"One day, after many nights of searching, Black Jet Woman finally appeared to her. She said she would give Wyunetta one answer and one promise. Wyunetta asked what she was supposed to do with her life, now that The One that was her baby girl was gone."

I lean forward in anticipation, savoring the story as surely as the meal Wyunetta had prepared for me only days before.

"Before Black Jet Woman answered the question, she changed into all four of her seasonal forms, to White Shell Woman of spring, then Turquoise Woman of summer, then Abalone Shell Woman of fall, and then back to Black Jet Woman. She said this was the promise, that just as the seasons change, so would Wyunetta's misfortune. Then Black Jet Woman answered her question. She said, 'What you dream in your heart is what the Great Goddess dreams for you. To hear wisdom you need only ask your heart what it wants most.'"

My storyteller is silent as he lets his story sink in. As it does, I slowly turn away from what is impossible and toward what I dream.

I look to the ever-darkening sky over the great crack of earth below, imagining Black Jet Woman crouching on her haunches in some cliff nearby. I've always said I wanted to help save the world. The only thing I wanted more was to be a mother. Now it seems they are one and the same.

I turn back to Nelson. "Kind of hard to turn away from your dreams being handed to you on a silver platter."

He tips his hat to me, like he's never questioned the outcome.

"I think I'm gonna go now," I say, but nothing happens. "How do I do this?"

"I'm not sure. Maybe open your eyes?"

"My eyes are open," I say.

"Your other eyes," he says, sounding distant, until all I hear is the drum, beating double-time.

I open my eyes to Chief, sitting next to me as I left him. I look to the sky, now fully night, littered with stars. I remember the Navajo say the stars hold the world together. Certainly they have been holding mine.

I'm back. Not a dream. A miracle. I was there. At the same time, I was here, all along.

"Now what?" I ask the precious one who is seeing me through, all the way.

He smiles, fully present. "You'll probably throw up."

29

There was no "probably" to it. My body shook, from a slow chill across my shoulders to a violent, full-body, near-epileptic revolt. My knees and teeth clenched in a vain attempt to issue some sort of self-control, until there was nothing left to do but give in to it, let it have its way with me, turning my insides out. Chief took it all in stride, putting twigs in the fire, as he does now.

"Why now?" I ask, now that my stomach has at least slowed its spasms and I am well enough to sit before the fire. "Why not ten years ago? You said before that we were late. Why did you make me wait so long?"

"I did come ten years ago," Chief explained. "In Tibet. Together we prostrated before the huge Buddha statue for a whole day."

I look at him blankly. "No. That was a monk. A Tibetan."

"That was me."

I think back. I only saw his face through the corner of my eye. Besides, I was zoned out, blitzed on bliss by the mere energy in the room.

"Yes. Yes! I felt the same way when we first met in the canyon. I remembered that moment. It was you in Tibet, too? Why didn't you approach me? Say something?"

"We talked," he says with a look that admits we did not talk at all, at least not with words. "We went outside of space and time. You were not ready."

"How do you know?"

He squats to look me in the eyes. "You told me."

"I didn't say a word! The whole day."

"Yes, but we conversed."

"And I said I wasn't ready? Why not?"

He moves again, putting water on for tea. "'You were not desperate enough. You had not yet seen enough Nothin'.'"

"Is that how it goes, you make a person desperate first, to get her to do what you want?"

"Of course not. You were not desperate enough to endure what you have so far. Certainly not enough to face the challenges that still lie ahead. Do you think that then, at age twenty-five, you could have endured all of this?"

No. No way.

I did want to save the world, even then. But I wouldn't have been able to face the insanity these journeys bring on. Without my travels and meeting the great teachers I have met, and without becoming more and more desperate, my mind would have completely balked at the very first journey to Kenya.

"Okay, point taken. But then, who are you really?" I feel I know, maybe have known all along, but it won't come clear. As if I block it for some reason.

"Name's Chief," he says.

"Come on. Don't you trust me yet?"

"I trust you with my life, Sweet Mary. I was supposed to die ten years ago, just after we met. I've been holding on, holding the dream for us both, waiting all this time for you to be ready. I held myself back from our meeting until there was no more time left. It is my trust in you, your innate hope, that has kept me dreaming. How could I not trust you? We are one."

"You keep saying that, but I don't know what it means." Another lie I have told to myself too long.

He stoops to look intently at me again, reflecting my own eyes back at me. I know what to do. I go deep into my center.

The understanding comes. On its heels, humility and awe.

"You! You are the Divine Incarnation of Love!" It's not a question. I know it. "You want to be born to me?"

"I cannot imagine a better mother."

Time stops as I hold his words close, lock them in, let them sweep my heart into oblivion as huge teardrops of joy spill, a sacred waterfall if ever there were one.

"I don't know if I am ready for that kind of honor."

"That is the whole point of these journeys. There are more still in front of you. Are you ready?"

"More journeys? Tonight?"

"My extended grace period in this body is quickly ending. If you wish me here as your guide, we must push on."

I laugh, unable to fathom where my strength will come from. Yet could I possibly make this amazing man wait another moment for our mission to progress? Will I allow one more ounce of hesitation to hinder our cause? Will I let him go before the outcome is assured? Not a chance.

I take a deep breath and nod "yes," my questions hounding me even as we begin the ceremonies. "So how do I know these journeys are real, or that I'm getting it right? What if it is all just some psychological projection tied to my warped imagination?"

"Again I say, nothing is real. Not the lifetimes you visit, or this one. Don't look for real. Look for meaningful. Does the story you find help you understand why you feel and act as you do? Does it help you consider where you might have put stumbling blocks in your own way? Real or unreal is beside the point entirely."

Just go with it, girl.

"Okay. You will tell me more, though, eventually, won't you? Because there is still so much I don't get."

"Remember your Taoist truth," he suggests as he lights the sage, "give up and you will succeed."

Okay, I give up. I'm not sure what success is. But if somewhere along the line a life with Chief is the prize, that is plenty good enough for me.

I enter the bliss of being smoked with sage by Love Incarnate, then make my way to the ground. Chief drums as though he has all the strength in the world.

If I'm dreaming, don't wake me up. Ever.

I allow myself to be seduced by the beat, finding the tree with the huge roots and going down, down. Lion appears. Perhaps it is my imagination, but I do believe she is smiling.

In the distance, I hear Dixieland music. This time, I do not fly over oceans, though there is a brief sensation of going backwards.

"Georgia, nineteen twenties," Lion offers without a prompt.

So I see. Plantation-style homes with cotton fields come into view, creating a romantic, "Gone With The Wind" feeling. Pecan trees sway, sending their scent on the wind. Below me, the women are dressed in full Southern skirts. All except one, dressed like a flapper. I don't have to look into her eyes, let alone lay my soul upon hers, to know she is me. Maybe it is because it is so recent—less than eighty years ago? I don't know. I move behind her eyes easily, our souls clinging together like magnets attracted to each other.

I relate easily to her—to her way of thinking, her flippant attitude, her broken heart under a bold exterior. Through her eyes, my soul gently merging with hers, I remember like it was yesterday.

An expansive veranda hosts half a dozen family members, all walking on eggs around me. I haven't been home in more than a year. Nobody's impressed with my style, though none can argue with my success. I've the "voice of a goddess," one reviewer said, soon to have the pocketbook of a queen. Assuming I don't keep preaching from my "nigger-lover" soapbox before and after my shows. Which, by God, I will so long as I have breath and opportunity.

"Have you seen him yet?" a young girl, not more than ten, asks me in a near whisper. Lilly, my little sister. Though more than a decade apart, she lights my life. Looking in her eyes, I see it is Hannah turned Puck.

Looking at her wheelchair, and deathly pale complexion, I know this lifetime is nearing an end for her. Why must it be so in every lifetime for this soul, and what does that mean for Puck this time around?

I shake my head once in answer to her question. Best not talk about it here. In the past it was hard to keep her from babbling on and on about what she could see, even when she knew she wasn't supposed to see it. Even when it was as dangerous as a white woman in love with a black man. Now the illness has taken away her exuberance.

"I told him you were coming," Lilly whispers.

Through my eyes back then, I picture who she is talking about. Ray. Son of a freed slave, yet still a slave to the economics of a black man in the South. He's worked here since he was old enough to carry water. I've loved him at least that long. Born on the same day of the same year, we've grown up together. Me, a rich white woman with every privilege. He the son of a former slave, born into poverty and little opportunity.

"You need to keep quiet young lady," I say, not too stern. "Trouble comes to those who play with the affairs of others."

Lilly looks crushed. I give her an assuring squeeze of the hand to let her know I am not really cross. She feels cold. So cold. I've stayed away too long. They say she was almost gone from us, coming back to life only when she heard I was planning a visit home. Though my work demands all of me, I will stay to the end. The doctors predict it soon enough.

"A certain someone," she continues so that only I can hear, "has been taking me to the cotton fields at night, to see the moon. Mamma lets me or I cry. He's taught me about God, and what to do when it hurts."

I would love to hear what she has learned. To hear what my beloved has to say about anything. It's been so long since we've had any real kind of conversation. I can only hope he knows why I left home, and him. Because I have a voice people want to hear, and a message that I pray will free him. I've no illusions we can be together. But for him to be truly free, that would be enough.

I pull away to look at Lion. "I'm still trying to make up for China, aren't I?"

Lion does not answer. I meld again with my Georgia self.

"Maybe tonight we can look at the moon ourselves," I say to Lilly.

I'd swear I see a twinkle in her eyes before she closes them and begins to breathe the breath of sleep as the rest of us look on, helpless to do anything but hush ourselves so as to give her peace.

Again I pull away, so easy in this lifetime. To be there and here, back and forth, in a split second. Is it the recent time, or am I getting better at these journeys? Either way, I can sense something coming, almost hear the bones cracking. I am surprised at how brave I feel.

"Forward, to the moonlight," Lion says, taking me into the evening without a hint of what is to come.

30

Georgia lays itself open wide under the night sky. Lilly has managed to get me here, in the field, and Ray too, though Mamma nearly had a fit with a dying child as my only escort. Both of my parents have always known, on some level, about my feelings for Ray. It was only Ray's firm resolve never to express what we feel in any physical way (at least no more than that one simple kiss behind the stables on a hot night in our teenage years) that has kept us safe from her finding a good enough reason to send him off to some other plantation.

My baby sister sits on my lap, as she so often did as a small child. Sadly, she doesn't weigh much more than she did in those early, robust days. Between her and Ray, my heart breaks again and again. It is only my passion for freedom that makes it all bearable.

Through the eyes of my Georgia self, I stare at Ray indirectly, enchanted both as the me I was and the me I am today. He is huge and bald, dark chocolate brown, with a gentle strength and a handsome face. How could anyone call a man like this "boy"? And yet they do. All day, every day.

I want to talk to him. Really talk. Yet he will not speak without being spoken to, knowing his place, even though it is just us. I can't remember when that started, only that once I realized it, there was no turning back. He is a man of honor and dignity. I love him for it, for living life on his own terms even within the prison he was born into, though I have never agreed it was right.

I watch Lilly, looking into the vast starry sky. In times past, she would have gone on and on about this star and that. Now, she just gazes. Does she know she'll be going to the stars soon? I don't want to ask.

"Sing for us," Lilly asks me.

I shake my head no, embarrassed. I can sing for the whole world, but in front of Ray? My voice would quiver and my knees knock.

Lilly seems to understand my hesitation. "He used to listen to you all the time, when you'd practice in the parlor."

"Is that so?" I ask, finally daring to look him in the eyes.

He is without expression. "You've a fine voice, ma'am," he says. "Lotsa folks do enjoy it."

I get a wonderful ripple of chills, just hearing his deep resonance. He might as well have kissed me while lying naked out in an open grassy field.

"You know why I left home to sing, don't you?" I question him. "For freedom. Real freedom for every black man and woman that lives. You do know that?"

"That's a dangerous thing to say out here, ma'am," he warns.

I know. I know about the Klan. And I know what happens when I go too far on any stage anywhere in the country, North or South. Already I've been blackballed by certain groups.

"Life is dangerous," I say to Ray directly. "I want you to be free, really free."

He sits, close enough to touch, still as a rock. "Only time I'se free is times I ain't thinkin'a you."

His words sting, but I've often thought the same thing. If I could just forget him, the longing would not tear at me, day and night, in every city, at every nightclub, whenever a black man hands me a glass of wine but won't speak unless spoken to.

Lilly moans, bringing me back to the cotton fields.

"Is it bad?" I say, taking her more fully in my arms.

"Tell her," she says to Ray with little breath, "what you told me about pain."

"Yes, tell me," I say, daring to touch his arm.

An electrical shock, visible in the night, flies between us. His arm flexes, then relaxes into my touch.

"Everybody got pain of some kind. Out here, it's cotton. Ya can't stop pickin', can't sit down. So's ya go into it, tha's all. Pain stops chasin' when ya stop runnin'. Still there, but it do stop its'a chasin'."

"I'm not running," Lilly says, her head heavy under my

chin.

My lip trembles, but I steady my voice. "I don't like the sound of that, Lilly. We don't want you giving up on us."

Ray pulls his arm from under my fingers to reach out and caress Lilly's face. I see now what friends they have become in my absence. "She'll be fine in the arms of our Lord Jesus," he says softly, reassuring her.

I pat her head, unable to stop the tears, just as unable to believe in his Lord. Wasn't Jesus about freedom? Then why, two thousand years later, isn't someone with faith such as his a free man?

"How do you know?" I ask him.

"I have faith," he says. Just like that.

You are Faith.

"I'm tired," Lilly says, sounding more than tired. Her breath is labored, her face ashen. I know what I cannot bear to know, that these are her last moments.

"Don't make me do this," I pull away to say to Lion. "Don't make me watch her die."

"Ray was right, it helps to go into the pain," Lion says.

"It was bad enough then, when it was only Lilly. Now she's Hannah and Puck, too. I can't bear that. I just can't. You said I'm in charge."

"So you are. Move forward, then."

I travel on, not going far. It is only days later. Lilly is buried, her grave dug by the large, silently weeping black man who carried her dead body back into the house later that night and laid it out, like a picked rose, on her own bed. My beautiful Ray.

Now, my Georgia self is at the edge of the property, giving him money, sending him off. He carries a small bundle tied to the hook of a hoe. It holds all he owns. I cannot bear to get close to this parting either, and so keep my soul at a distance, only watching.

"This will get you North, and last you a little while after," my Georgian self says.

His head is hung, though it is hard to say if it is in shame for taking the money, or grief at leaving the woman he loves. I can't bear to consider either.

"I want you to be free," she adds. "Really free. So you stop thinking of me. Forget me. Use that faith of yours and ask God to wipe any trace of me from your mind."

He touches my fingers as he takes the money. "I'm beholden to you, ma'am," he adds. She knows he means so much more than the money.

"No you're not. You're free. That's the whole point. If that is all I can give, I will give you that."

He looks up and into her face, not a "boy" but a man. A man with a heart. "What can I give ta you?" he asks.

She shakes her head and turns up the drive, heading to the veranda where she pours herself a stiff drink, never looking back. The booze is down her in one large gulp. As she pours the next, I see a ghostly image of her soul rise up. It traipses off to curse up a storm in the cotton fields of her great loss. Like a broken record, the ghost replays again and again the sweetest words she would ever hear:

"You've a fine voice, ma'am. Lotsa folks do enjoy it."

Above, I hear the drum beat go into double-time. I find my way back to ordinary reality and open my eyes to a huge full moon. The fire is only embers.

"Did he do it? Did he forget me?" I ask Chief.

Chief nods nails into my heart. "Too well. He prayed day and night, as you requested, to give you what you wanted. Being the Divine Incarnation of Faith, there was no way for his prayers to go unanswered. He not only forgot you as his true love in that life, but you forever. You as Norbu, and so himself, and me as well."

I knew he was gone. Have always known it. That hole in my heart.

"Where is he now? I know he's not here. If his soul was anywhere on this earth, I'd know it."

"You are right," Chief agrees. "With no pain to keep him attached to this world, he became his full essence and ascended."

"Ascended? You mean, like an ascended Master?"

He lays down his drum and begins to the stoke the fire. "Something like that," he replies. "Not that it is doing any of us any good."

31

Chief offered me no further explanation of Ray's ascended status before making himself tea and sending me off to sleep. A healing journey would be taken in the morning, he said. I would need my rest. I needed no convincing. As I drifted off, thoughts of Ray, finally free, gave me a joy unsurpassed.

Now, as the sun shines bright on a new day, my courage is renewed. As is my ever expanding list of questions. Why are we even discussing Ray, if he is already arrived where all men long to go? Will I fly to some place in the heavens, and return pregnant by The Essence Of Ray? Please, let it be more down to earth than that.

"So many questions," Chief says, obviously hearing my thoughts.

"You do realize," I ask, "that every time you answer one question, you bring on a thousand more?"

Chief smiles. "There are worlds between worlds, worlds inside of worlds, worlds beyond worlds. The more you learn, the less you know. The wise do not fight this, only stand in amazement."

I don't ask him about the contradiction that I am to know what I know. I have a feeling the answer to that would spin yet another web of questions I will want more answers to.

"Yet there are things we have to do," I argue instead. "I don't even know what they are. What about those questions? The nuts and bolts?"

"I repeat, every answer is inside you. Ask your questions, but look for answers within yourself."

"But I don't trust my answers!"

"Ah, well," he says, shrugging as if that says it all.

"I trust you," I add.

"Again, we are one and the same."

"Yes, but you're double strength."

"If I tell you the sky is blue twice, does that make it any more blue?"

"You're playing word games with me. I only want to know what I need to, so I can do what I came to do. Isn't that what you want?"

"I want you to trust yourself. To believe that you do have all the answers. Not only that, but also the power to change the answers you don't like."

"How do I come to believe that?"

"A healing journey," he says, pointing to the small pouch around my neck, the one Maria gave me in the Amazon. I touch it, remembering the promise that came with it. One day, she said, I would return to her for a teaching contained in the pouch. It was not meant to be.

"Stones, from a shaman I once met. She died soon after."

"Death has no finality. She will meet you, as promised. Look inside."

I take the pouch from my neck. Maria had warned me not to look inside until I was ready for its contents. She said I would know when, and before that time it would only make me question too much. I smile to myself, knowing she was right about both the questioning and my knowing when. I am certain the time is now.

My neck feels weak and exposed without the stones. Have I come to depend on them so much? In my excitement, I pull at the leather lacing, tightened over the years, so that my fingers begin to redden in my struggle to get at it.

"Let go," Chief says.

I lay the pouch down as told, heaving out a frustrated sigh.

"Now, open the pouch and let go at the same time," he says.

"How?"

"Allow it. Allow it to open, believing it wishes to be opened, because it does. Everything you want, wants you, too. That is universal law. Yet nothing wishes to be forced. When you force a thing, anything, even only with your mind, you invoke its resistance. That is the polarity of earth, the hot and the cold, the up and the down of things. Desire it and there is no resistance."

I pick up the pouch, let out a breath, then another. Why shouldn't it work this way—the things I want, also wanting me? After all, I traveled the world, searching a hundred ways to Sunday for my destiny with this great Chief. And all the while, he was dreaming of me, for me. I begin to play with the lacing, easing, probing, tossing, allowing. Yet it remains tight.

"At this rate, we'll be here all night," I complain.

"Let go of your need for when. When does not matter. Time is only an invention for the sake of organizing experiences."

I listen to his sing-song voice, wooing me as I work. I let go a breath and begin massaging the lace, allowing a small opening to appear, working it gently.

"How can we be ten years late, then?" I ask, this time without demand, a simple wanting to know, imagining that since I want the answer, the answer must want me.

"Inside this world here, time is part of the game. It would have been best for our work together here to have occurred ten years ago. It did not, so we are ten years beyond the optimal date for you to have found Ray, brought him back and begun your courtship."

"Doesn't that sort of sink the ship right there?"

"Not at all. Outside of this lifetime experience, this earth, there is no time. We will simply go outside of time to jump into time at a different point. No real problem, except that the body I am in is quickly deteriorating, so if you wish my guidance from here, we must get on with our work."

I continue to breathe softly, calmly allowing my hands to work open the pouch, make the small hole bigger, and ask what I want to know.

"Do you mean Kenya will alter the past for us?"

"She has already given me ten years in this old body, and she will continue to assist us. Her efforts will be fueled by the force I have created by dreaming a new dream these past ten years. That is another reason I do not sleep. I spend my sleeping hours consciously dreaming the life that would have occurred if we were on schedule. In non-ordinary reality, out of space and time, that dream is as real as this one. In it, I've already been born, to you and my father, Ray. I am seven years old."

"Is that like a parallel reality?" I ask, focusing on Chief's aura instead of his words. His words take me into sci-fi weirdness, but his aura is peaceful, keeping me calm.

"Every dream is a reality, at some level. I have infused this dream with a great deal of energy, designing every detail, which brings it life. Assuming all goes as I plan—since I cannot control you as a separate entity here on earth, that is up to you—we will jump into this new life when the time is right."

"Time again?" I question, still not getting it.

"Time is a reality here. We cannot deny its laws, being in its jurisdiction. We can only change the rules outside of ordinary reality."

"Like getting married in Vegas, then flying home to D.C.?"

"Exactly right," Chief says. "See how much you know when you allow?"

With this, the pouch falls open, revealing the gems I have long sought. Stunned at what lies before me, I am knocked clean out of my "allowing" state of mind.

"Holy shit," I say, because it looks more like shit than any kind of gem.

32

"I don't believe it," I sputter, looking at the dark green, grossly shaped nuggets in my pouch. "These aren't stones. They're drugs."

I remember them from Maria's psychotropic plant spirit journeys. Heated and then mixed with lots of spit, the ghastly concoction sent her flying into the place where she worked miracles. She had always encouraged me to partake, to learn to fly like the shaman she insisted I was. As a professional observer, a scientist—not to mention one who is smart enough to avoid another's spit—I always refused. I wonder now, had I had the courage then, would we be only five years late instead of ten?

I look at the small nuggets.

"I can't believe I've been wearing an illegal substance around my neck all these years. I've traveled through so many airports."

The idea begins to panic me. "I could have been nailed to the wall. Spent a lifetime in a foreign prison. I can't believe Maria would put me at such risk!"

"No risk," Chief says, "when you believe that what you are wearing is just a bag of stones. Not knowing, you did not resist. Not resisting, there was nothing to fear. No fearing, no problems."

I laugh. Unbelievable. Impossible. Like the rest of this blessed journey.

"Now we will make the mixture for you to drink. You will fly out of ordinary reality, even further than you have gone."

"Uh," I say, knowing how lame I'm going to sound even before I start. "Listen, Chief, these kind of drugs, they can really knock you out. Send you to la-la land staring at your own fingers for days at a time. In fact, I happen to know for a fact that they can kill you. Can't I just go with the drumming? I was getting good at it."

Chief offers me a loving gaze, enough to warm even my hard heart. "Your resistance is still so high. Even with this ally, there is no certainty you will be able to get past it and do what you must."

"Well, are you at least sure they are safe?"

"Life is not safe," he says, repeating the theme of my journey to Georgia. "But you are ready."

His words shake me. Ten years ago, I was not ready. Will I say that to him again? Will I go against what Maria told me about my being a shaman, too? Will I go against what even I, deep down, have longed to do—fly beyond time as the shamans must?

"Okay," I agree before I can stop myself.

Minutes later, a bowl of warm Chief spit and Maria's plant is offered to me. I look into it, sniff a pungent odor. My hands shake at the bowl, my first "food" in days. Chief must have known this was coming, too. Maria would not eat for days before she journeyed. The retching was hard enough on an empty stomach. Considering what mine has been through with the bi-locating, I'm thankful not to even have shared tea with Chief last night.

Looking at the mixture, I consider all who have come before me, joining with the plant world to find other worlds. I lift the bowl to my lips. The strange bitterness of the first drop sends me gagging, so that I must force my stomach not to revolt as the rest goes down. My mouth grows hot inside, burning fire, and my eyes water in a steady stream.

Chief takes the bowl and puts his hands on my shoulders, laying me down to await my trip. With perfect bedside manner, he holds my hand. No drumming this time. He is needed at my bedside.

I want to ask what I am to look for, but when I open my mouth, I can only laugh. I don't feel like laughing, I feel like vomiting. Yet I laugh. I had not expected the poison to attack so soon. Am I not supposed to throw up? How can I, if I can't even move? If I don't, it will kill me. I laugh again until it starts to come up. Chief turns me to my side as I heave, burning my throat as the evil exits. My stomach pumps like a machine, blow after blow. There is nothing to give up but the drink, yet it goes on forever, heave upon heave. Chief stays with me.

When at last I return to my back, Chief is over me, speaking, though I cannot hear. His mouth moves slowly. I do not understand anything except what he has tried to teach me all along. That we are one.

I melt into the ground, one with the ground. I look into the stars, one with the stars. I feel my tongue in my mouth, heavy and lethargic, wanting to speak not for me, but with me. Like an entity unto itself, my tongue doesn't like the way I swear. I reply wordlessly that I'm sorry, I never thought of my tongue having an opinion in the matter. I promise to work on it. My tongue thanks me for the consideration and leaves my direct consciousness.

I begin to float, up, away, and down, inside, all at once. Beyond here or there. A green and blue globe of the earth is before me, split in half to open like a cracked egg. I go into the crack and find another, smaller world in the distance. I fly to it, now huge. It, too, cracks open. Inside and inside and inside again, until I am a dozen worlds into the world, finally stopping in pitch dark, standing with one foot on a high, high pole, no wider than a flagpole, but much higher. Worlds high. I don't know how to get down. Terror fills me as strange birds fly in bizarre patterns, screeching at me like demons.

I'll never get down. Never get back.

Before me, suspended in dark mid-air, Maria appears.

What relief!

Oh, friend, how long it has been! How much I have wanted to journey to you. I meld into her and out again, at one with the Universe she is.

"Good stuff, huh?" she says with a great laugh.

"I always liked you, Maria. Everybody loved you for your miracles, but I liked you because you were funny. You never took even your miracles too seriously."

"Simple magic. Shoulda rubbed off on you, shaman girl!" she says. "No mind now—Maria is here!"

"Just like you promised. I didn't know it was still possible, after you died. I'd have come sooner."

She waves off my apologies. "You wanna get a healing?"

"Yes," I say in all earnest.

"Good!"

I remember now how fast we had become friends, how much she had given to me in the short time we walked together through the rain forests, where everything was alive. Really alive. I begin to weep for how little I could appreciate what I was experiencing at the time. The tears fall into the dark nothingness that surrounds us, glittering like diamonds.

"Let's go," she says, swooping me up under one arm like a superhero. Colors explode as we whoosh along, hues and textures I have never seen before, making me sick. I know I am vomiting again, back there, where the illusion of life is. The colors turn gray and dark green, like the ugly concoction I have eaten.

Regret for my decision to partake swallows me into the drab palate. I lose my equilibrium, my sense of direction. I am plucked out of Maria's hold, swimming in putrid colors, the smell of a river of waterlogged dead rats envelops my senses.

"This way," she says from somewhere else.

I cannot follow, flung like a bug in a tornado. The gray-green overwhelms me, taking on faces of the sewer rats, the same ones that seem to be passing through my throat as I heave.

Maria finds me, lost in my own innards.

"Here, little shaman girl!" she says, sticking me on another pole, this one to ride like a witch's broom. She straddles her own and I follow suit. Side by side, we fly into a moonless night, clean and clear, until the darkness becomes lit by the brilliance of a thousand stars.

Here, between stars, I am smack dab in the middle of pure intelligence. Ah! This is it! This is why I love to think. Because thinking is also divine. Understanding a joyous quest, so long as the Oneness is not forgotten.

I laugh and laugh, flying, truly. Ho ho! I like this trip.

"More drugs, please," I say, like Oliver requesting more gruel, winking at Maria, then bending over, laughing myself silly.

When at last I upright myself, I see several iridescent pillars of light, pulsing with life. Though faceless, I know they are looking at me. They have no emotions, yet they seem to offer me thoughts of beauty, a kind of regal affirmation that reflects ideas beyond that which my mortal body can understand. I sense the message clearly. I am doing a good job. I laugh, then whiz past on my magic pole and salute them. In response, they pulse out stunning geometric light forms that seem to me like lesson plans. I fly into the forms and learn, propelled by Divine Intelligence.

So, this is it.

This is unity.

This is now.

This is allow.

This is everything in perfect time.

No way to be off track.

No way to mess up.

No reason to worry, ever.

I feel the pulse, a stunning light show, a celestial rain become manifest. My diamond tears are gathered into a new pouch to wear about my neck. My tears, I feel them communicate, will help purchase the world's freedom.

Yes! Yes! A freedom fighter! That is what I have always been. What Hope hopes for. Everything in my life back there makes sense, one truth hitting another, like dominoes set off, falling into one another in chain reaction.

"I want to look at earth through the lens of this understanding," I tell Maria.

Together we ride our poles into the rain forest. I see myself, all those years ago. How small I look, how afraid. Yet the trees are alive, producing oxygen, the life force of mankind, as I saw them in my first journey. While we rape them, ignorantly pillaging our own life, they serve as ever-giving wisdom keepers. I weep for the beauty of it, and the destruction of that beauty, and to know I have been a part. More diamonds for my pouch.

In them, I see my own reflection. I am the tree, and the destroyer, the animal chasing her own tail. It is the knowing we avoid at all costs and search for at the same time. That all things are one.

All One.

Finally, I get it. I am The One, because we all are The One. So simple.

Maria appears in front of me. "Having fun?"

"Yes! And ready to be on with it. What now, my friend?" I ask, feeling for the first time that Maria, like Chief, is no wiser than I. Only more informed.

She points me toward a spot on the horizon. I follow it.

Ireland again.

In the flash of a lightning streak, we arrive at the time and place where Dark Crow is killing me and my baby. From this distance, I see why it is so. It is not time for me to have a child. When Hope has a child, Love comes. The world is not ready, but there is all the time in the world. I see that now. Yet the Irish woman I once was does not know. She feels only the trauma. In the corner, I see the ghost that lifted from her, frantic and grieving.

"Heal yourself," Maria says.

I do not have to ask what she means.

I approach the form, the ghostly shadow, knowing, finally, what has occurred. It was here, in this juxtaposition of space and time, that I allowed my fear to keep a portion of my soul. That place inside that had confidence in my ability to protect my child. Now, I must reunite with her, bring her back to Mary Margaret, so the child can at last be born.

"Hello!" I say to the ghost of my soul. "Come this way, I will show you amazing things!"

She looks at me, only half seeing, and shakes her head nervously.

What? She does not want me? Now, when I can see it all? Impossible.

I swoop down to her again, smiling into her face. "Look, I will show you how good it gets, come with me!"

I whiz past and look back to see her still uncertain. Clearly, this enticement will not work. I slow myself, listen to the knowing that I know. Ah, so this is who she is. Not interested in anything but her baby, lying cold in the womb of the dead woman on the floor. I approach slowly, this time with compassion.

"The baby is not dead," I say softly.

She looks up at me.

"It was not the baby's time, but the time is coming, soon. A great teacher, this baby will be. Come with me. We will find the baby together."

She looks at me with wide eyes and distrust. "You are too flippant. Too crass. You will never make a good mother."

What? Is this what I think? What I fear? Too flippant, too crass to be a good mother?

Yes, I realize. It is true. But only because the good mother in me was left here in the form of a ghost. This, I see, is my fuel, the power I need to convince her to return to me.

"The child will come, one way or the other. Yet without you, I cannot be the mother you would have been. If you return to me, we can mother this child together."

She is thinking about it, wondering if I mean it.

"The child deserves a whole mother," I say, shameless in my sales pitch, yet believing what I say. Without another word, she eases onto my pole, sliding forward and into me, merging souls, like a shadow becoming one with its source. A gentleness overcomes me, greater than any I have known in this life. My compassion, at last, feels as if it has a place within me, a place to reside beyond an idea in my head. This is the wholeness I have sought.

I swoop out of Ireland, more me than I have ever been, accomplishing my own healing. Maria joins up with me, laughing. I don't have to ask her what is next. I know where I am going.

33

The lightning flashes and below I see the volcano, smell the sulfur mixed with lush, moist earth. In front of me, my own ghost is flying like a bird. Maria eases off, leaving me to my work. I speed up to catch the lost fragment of my soul.

"Hello! Remember me?" I ask, wondering how I will convince this one.

She catches my eye, then looks away, lost in the peace of her flight.

"I've come to bring you home," I say.

"I am home," she says, trying to sound serene. I recognize the force behind her words. Trying to be at peace, trying to be enlightened, trying, ever trying. And under it all, pure fear. That's me, all right.

"I need you to come with me. I have a mission."

"Call on the wise Kahuna there," she replies with sarcasm, motioning to the volcano's edge. "He will help you."

"Him?" I laugh. "He is not wise. I know him today, in my current life. He is full of Nothin'. But he still has it in for me. I need you, your intuition, to keep him from getting me again, as he has so many times."

She looks as if she is considering my suggestion.

"You do me no good floating out here, avoiding the pain. I need you to be fully present with me. I need to believe in your gifts again, to be able to know what I know and be all of who I came to be. To help free my people just as you wanted to free yours."

"What about Lono? My god has abandoned me. How can I help you without his manna?"

"Forget the gods. You are a goddess in your own right. If you had realized you could use your own manna, perhaps you would have seen, in advance, what was coming and made changes to avoid it."

"I knew it. You blame me. I am guilty. Too guilty to help you."

So, even more of that self-blame I am so famous for. Stuck here, in a ghost of my own soul. How do I work with that? Like magic, Hannah's face appears before mine. I know what to say.

"We must give up guilt." I repeat my beloved's own wisdom to me from so long ago. A riveting current of ecstasy flows through me as I fully understand her wise words for the first time. "Not the guilt which would guide us to do right, but the guilt that makes us feel unworthy and so keeps us from attempting anything truly great."

"Do you really think there is still a chance?" she asks, sounding as though she dares not hope, and yet cannot help herself. Like me. She is Hope.

"Yes. Many people have come to help us. We are not alone. Will you bring your Divinity back to us, or stay out here as the bird, free and easy, but doing no good?"

"That is not my intention!"

"Then come with me. Please."

"Promise me, first, that you won't let that evil one near us."

I don't like the idea of making promises to anyone, even myself. Not after my costly, misguided promise to Hannah. "I promise I will try. Your being a part of me again will help."

She shows her agreement by gliding onto my pole, sliding up into me until again, I am reunited with myself. I feel heavy in the best of ways, as if my soul has put on hiking boots.

"Doing good!" Maria affirms, appearing next to me. "Now China."

With that, I balk.

"No," I say, knowing I am in charge. "I'm not ready. I need to gather more strength. Georgia first."

"Okay," Maria shrugs, "but the big power is in China."

I don't want to think about that. Even here, flying with all that is One, where wisdom comes ten insights at a time, I can't fathom going back there. Can't imagine letting that horrible, small self I was back into my soul. Why? With a soul like that, who needs enemies?

"Georgia," I say, and we are there, pecan trees and cotton fields, long elegant verandas, and my ghost, drunk as a skunk before noon. I fly down on my pole, swooping past. I catch my ghost's attention, smile at her, ask her if she'd like to go for a ride. She seems uninterested, wanting to wallow in her drink.

No wonder I failed to thrive as Wyunetta's child. A part of me was still three sheets to the wind. I swoop past again, suggesting I might have something she wants. Unless it is a drink, she's not interested. Her true love is gone. What else is there to live for? Besides, she knows the only way out is through the pain, and she has long ago decided she is not going there.

What to do? A knowing comes quickly, my Hawaiian intuitive self already helping me see. We will need a special ally.

I swoop past my surroundings, not only in Georgia, but out here, in the worlds between worlds. Off in the distance, I see a coyote. A trickster. Ah, so a trickster is needed. I follow the coyote, but he ignores the stupid human I am completely. I turn myself into a coyote and walk with him, our legs trotting in unison.

"I need help," I plead. He gives no reply.

Be the coyote, I say to myself, willing it to be. I feel him, feel his movement and his motivation. "Want to be a trickster?"

He turns to me and grins, fangs exposed, replying in singsong: "What do you do with a drunken sailor? What do you do with a drunken sailor? What do you do with a drunken sailor, early in the morning?"

"Exactly," I reply. "What *do* you do with a drunken sailor?"

He stops, as if thinking, then lifts a leg to pee on a bush.

At first I just wait, then I catch on. Wet her down! My drunken singer needs a good dousing to sober her up. I will need sacred water, though. Where?

The waterfall! I fly through time to a day when the waterfall is flowing, so full of beauty. I imagine a bucket in my hands, and one appears. I fill it and go back to toss it on my drunken ghost.

It sobers her instantly.

"There's more where that came from if you don't help me," I threaten.

"Leave me alone you bitch!" she screeches, tossing an empty bottle of gin at me. So, this is why I can't give up swearing? The habit is stuck in the soul of a pissed-off drunk.

"Can't do that. You have something I need."

"I don't have anything anyone needs," she replies.

I hear myself in her words, but have had enough of that lie.

"I know what I know," I tell her. "You still want to fight for freedom, but you'll never do it here. Your voice has been silenced. Come with me, I'll help."

She eyes me as if she's taking a white glove to a mantle and finding it in sore need of a dusting. "What for? This world is a God-forsaken place, now that he is gone."

"We will find him and convince him to return," I retort, not knowing of my own intentions until I have voiced them. It gives me a jolt of hope so strong, I nearly fall off my pole.

"Leave him be!" she yells, protective to the core. "He's free."

I know I believe this, deep down in my bones. But here, in the unity of all that is, I have another perspective. "Is he free? Really? If we are all truly one, can any soul be free while forgetting the rest of the suffering world?"

She looks as if she is considering the idea, then waves me off. "Won't change a damn thing anyway. The Lillys of the world will still die."

I see this for what it is. My clue. My in.

"I know Lilly, today. She lives. I can take you to her."

This perks her up. "What do you mean?"

"I mean we live more than one lifetime. I am you, in the future. Lilly is alive again. Her name is Puck. She's the most beautiful five-year-old. A little boy this time. Full again of all that bubbly essence that makes everything a joy."

"I remember that," she says wistfully.

"I swear she lives. But she's in trouble. She needs us. Come back to me, and I'll have what it takes to help. We'll make it work for all of us."

I don't know where this confidence comes from, but I speak with conviction.

She stands, shaky, and walks over. "For Lilly," she says, jumping not on the pole, but directly into me. My piss and vinegar confidence has returned full force.

"For the Lillys of the world!" I shout, a battle cry.

Maria appears, pointing toward China.

"No, Maria," I say. "I don't need to go there now. I have my motherhood, my intuition, and my kick-ass southern belle back. Anything I left in China can stay there."

"Good," a man's voice says from behind me, "then I still have a job."

Dark, ugly, small. I know the voice. Dark Crow. Out here, on the wind.

"Go away!" I shout, not willing to turn around. I hear no more, and feel he has disappeared. At long last.

"See, Maria? There's more than one way to skin a cat."

She shakes her head. "Hubris of the gods. Now you gotta go to the future."

"Why?"

"To plant a seed you're gonna need."

Anything but China.

I swoop forward, hit a patch of something that sends me hydroplaning into time. Below me, the canyon. Dark Crow's filthy truck. Me inside. His pants are half down. He is edging toward my shoved up skirt and his fist is in the air. It is the shattering of the cheek that I intuited. Everything is going in slow motion.

"This," I gasp, "this is in my future?"

"Is now. Plant a seed," Maria instructs.

"I don't know what you are talking about."

"A seed. When this happens, this moment, what you gonna do?"

Dark Crow's hardness stares out at me like a huge, venomous snake. I can't think straight.

"I don't know!" I scream, sinking again, out of the beauty of the Oneness, into the horrors of living in reality.

"Heal yourself now, before you get there," Maria suggests.

"I don't know how," I bellow.

Hearing myself, I know I will never know how in this state of mind.

Relax. Breathe. Let go.

Clarity lands like a butterfly on my shoulder. As if the understanding has always been there, just waiting to be known, I see what I must do. I plant a seed by whispering into my own ear.

Maria offers a small smile, as if only partially satisfied. "Good to see you, little shaman girl."

I smile back, suddenly tired. I feel myself floating, back there, back into the reality of time and space. My eyes flutter open.

Chief is no longer sitting next to me, but lying on the dirt earth, looking far more tired than I. I squint, sit up, making sure I am really back, and not off someplace else or split again. My head is woozy, my stomach worse.

It doesn't matter. I've never seen Chief look like this, so small and old, even worse than when he took on my boil. I close my eyes tight, open them again. His eyes are blinking closed, his glow all but gone.

"No!" I cry out, pulling myself firmly into the present. I gently shake him by his bony shoulders. His body is limp, easy to maneuver. "You can't go yet!"

He coughs, serene. "I promised to meet the Holy People at Spider Rock. You must take me there."

34

Breaking camp is an easy task. Chief has walked softly on the land. Two bedrolls, a few cups and bowls, some extra clothing, all of which I take in small trips up the hand and toe holds, into the back of the cave within the canyon wall. No one will know it is here, besides me. In any event, my intuition is clear. I see myself returning to this camp at some point.

"Will we need your sacred bundle and drum?" I ask.

Chief shakes his head. In this, I know for sure what we are doing. Making our own long walk to the place where Chief wishes to die.

I try to comfort myself that for him to be born to me, he must die. A logical conclusion, though if we are to be making miracles with time, is it too much to ask that I don't have to witness his passing?

The work keeps me occupied. I feel a reverence, a great gratitude for these days in the Lion's Mouth. It has been quite a trip.

Chief looks to the sky once again. He seems to see beyond the pure blue and snowy white clouds of late afternoon, to the stars and their configurations hidden by the light. Did he know, all along, we had only days to work? Have I learned enough?

"You will have to carry me," he says, his legs weak and shaking beneath him as he makes his way to rest against a large rock.

I think for a moment, then go back up into the rock to get a single sheet. I measure it to him, knot it and slip it over one shoulder, tied at my middle. I tug on it, making sure it is secure, before I load my precious cargo. It holds.

Lifting Chief into my makeshift sling, he is nothing more

than bones upon my back. He edges in, working with me. The knot digs at my waist. He slings one arm over my shoulder and the other around my middle, then leans his body weight into me. His heart pressed to my back and legs dangling out the sling, skinny and awkward, we are ready. I concentrate on my balance, on the miles ahead, on walking without jamming his knees into my side or bouncing him too much.

I walk toward the setting sun. As if the whole of nature were supporting this walk, the wind blows at a low constant and the trees seem to bend in our favor. Turkeys, badgers and horned toad lizards all appear, quietly watching as we pass. Only now do I see how little of the land I have noticed during my stay here. As amazing as it is, Chief was my great draw. His face the only thing I wanted to look upon.

Though I breathe deeply so as not to panic, I am bombarded by question after question. What now? How are we to do this? Will he go to Ray, somewhere On High, and plead our case? Is there anything I can do to help him in his passing? What am I to do with his body once he has left it? Will I need to journey somewhere to "jump time," or is that possibility behind us now that his death is so near and I am still so ignorant? If I am to journey, who will drum for me? Most important, do I need to know any of this? Or will it all just play out, because Chief has dreamed it so and I agree?

I hesitate to ask my questions. He wants me to find my answers within. I'm just not sure I'm ready. "You okay back there?" I ask gently, trying to make my voice sound like a caress.

"A little tired," he replies. I slow my walk to readjust him to my frame and then press on. I feel the need to keep him talking. So long as he is talking, we have time to make it to Spider Rock.

"Why were you in an asylum?" I ask. Not an important question, something I can live with knowing or not knowing. Something I can hold loosely. Allow.

"I could not incarnate at full vibration without you as my mother. The electric shock provided by the asylum allowed more of my essence to join me." He speaks as though it is no big deal, just a way to do what needed to be done.

"A rough way to go about it," I comment.

"It was not pleasant," he agrees, though it does not sound like a complaint.

"So is giving birth to you going to feel like that for me?"

"It is already done. Remember, I am born. Seven years ago. It was a challenge, as I recall."

"Everything is a challenge with you," I reply, smiling.

"Yes."

I stop to readjust him again.

"So if I do this jump, I won't really be pregnant with you, will I?"

"You will remember giving birth to me as though the memory were yours."

"But it didn't really happen, except in your dream."

"None of our memories really happened. They are all about yesterday. Yesterday is a fabrication, as is tomorrow. Only now is real. My dream or yours, my memories or yours, none of it really matters. You will not know the difference."

"So will I forget? All this? My life these past ten years? Our time together?"

He chuckles. "With your tenacity, you'll probably hold on to the memory, at least some of it, for a short while. Even if you do, once you sleep again, you will not be able to hold on. The new life will take over, new memories replace the old. It is best this way. Otherwise, two sets of memories would drive you insane. Certainly it would cause a great hardship for Ray to remember the peace of where he comes from. I expect he will choose not to remember at all."

"I guess that is why we forget where we really come from, and that it is all an illusion in the first place."

"Yes. Once you fully realize it is only a game, the game is up."

"Self-realization," I say, thinking of all the Masters who have touted it. "But is that true for everyone, all humans? Or only me in my story?"

"For you, there is only your story," he answers. "If people would live their own story alone, do what their own dreams lead them to do, living would be so much easier. There would be no war. People would not need to force their beliefs on another in an attempt to make themselves secure in what they want to believe but are not certain of."

"What about the Dark Crows of the world? Can we leave them to know what they know? To their darkness?"

"What did Dark Crow say when he appeared to you in your healing journey?"

I think back, shuddering to even remember him. "He said he was glad to have a job, I suppose because I would not go back to China to bring back that part of my soul."

"Yes."

"But that makes no sense to me. Why would I want to take back that wretched part of my soul? Am I not here to evolve past such horrors?"

"You are here to be who you are. No more, no less. We all have darkness in us. It is the human condition. We all have light. When we deny any part of our self, we lose the power to choose which aspect of ourselves to act upon. We deny our darkness, assume we have gotten rid of it, as if we put the animal out the back door and that is all there is to it. Yet the animal is not gone. It is still there, hounding us from outside until we bring it back in, love it and tame it to our own liking. You cannot control an animal you put outside. Inside, it can be tamed."

"You're saying Dark Crow is my darkness, put outside?"

"Yes. He has a job because you gave it to him. He carries your darkness to you, again and again, until you can love your whole self."

"So what do I do with him now?"

"As I have said, if you want to help save the world, save yourself. Take back your own darkness, starve Dark Crow of his work and power. Once all is in balance, all is safe from the extreme of the pendulum swing."

I think on this for a time.

"So, that is how I sold my soul? Not the light of my soul, but the darkness?"

"Yes, Sweet Mary."

My heart swells to hear him call me that again.

"You see. You are touched when I call you "sweet." Yet you know you are not all sweet. So how can you be truly loved by me? Can you be fully loved by anyone who only wishes to see you as sweet?"

"You do not really love me?" I ask, wanting to stop, let him down, look him in the eye. But I have found a stride, and I am determined, whether he loves me or not, to bring him to his Holy People.

"I play a role. A role you have assigned to me. To see you as sweet and beloved. As you have assigned Dark Crow a role. To carry the darkness for you, make it external to you, so that you could say that you are not dark as well as light. Thus, you will love me, and hate him. But it is all only reflections of you, the beauty and the darkness you have denied, put outside. All pieces of you."

I walk on, unable to comprehend it all, knowing that if his plan works, I will lose what he has taught me anyway.

"Do not worry. You have the rest of this lifetime, at least, to discover these truths again. I will be with you."

If I can make this jump in the first place. I start to panic, seeing Spider Rock in the distance. There is still so much I don't understand.

"How am I to make this jump? Is there some ritual, some journey? And what about Ray? How does he come to remember us? What if he doesn't agree? Will you go to him when you...make your journey?"

"The death process entails many formalities. I will be busy. There are council meetings, higher beings who must review my plans for the jump. Everything required of any new incarnation. You will have to find Ray. One look upon your face, and he will remember."

"Me, find him? How? Do you have more of Maria's plant medicine?"

"You will need an even more powerful ally than that."

"Where do I find this ally?"

"In death," he says, like a punch line.

I do not like the sound of that at all. "What do you mean?"

"I mean that you are going to die with me."

35

Spider Rock came too quickly. The closer we got, the weaker Chief grew, coughing, speaking slowly, catching his breath between words. He spoke briefly of the power of the death ally and how, should our plan fail, I would not die, but only have had a near-death experience. If I passed my final test, all would be accomplished by morning. We would be dreaming an entirely different dream. I'd be a mother, married to my true soul mate. If I failed, I'd simply wake up, him dead at my side. He warned me the trip would take a lot out of me. I might be disoriented for a while.

I did not speak. I did not tell him of the future I had seen for myself in my last journey, with Dark Crow in the filthy truck and the seed I planted. Nor of my sense earlier in the day that I would be back at camp. If my intuition was on target, then I have already failed my test and this jump of time Chief has dreamed for so many years. I could only hope his telepathy was weakened. I did not want him to know of this failure as he prepared to die.

Instead, I called upon the Hope that I am, and the void where all new hope is created. In it, I sent a message to Kenya: "Transfer Request. The reality I am living is no longer acceptable to me."

Not by a long shot.

Now, on the far side of the great rock, Chief lies down, motioning me to lie next to him. I look for the Holy People he says have been waiting for us. None in sight. At least my sight. But the energy of the place is evident. The fifty-some-odd buzzards in the distance are reacting, frantically riding the thermal winds in a helix pattern, like they know something is up.

With sunset approaching, the sky is striking in its ever-changing variations of pink and blue, purple and white. It is something, something indeed, to know you are about to die. Everything becomes acutely precious. Nothing so precious, though, as the beloved man beside me.

"If this is a dream, my Chief Of No Tribe," I say quietly, "then you are the best dream I ever dreamed."

In response, he lifts a shaking, bony hand and rests it on mine. Without warning, we catapult into the air, he shooting farther and faster than I.

Into darkness, the void, blacker than the blackest bottom of the sea, darker than the depths of Mother Earth's core. Not into my psyche, or out into the Universe, but beyond space and time. No time. No place. The Void.

Peaceful. So peaceful. I am aware, yet out of my body completely.

Could it have happened so fast?

A moment there, on the earth, then not there anymore?

Dead, I guess. But where am I?

Instantaneous light, brilliant beyond brilliant, surrounds me, sucking me through a tunnel of living consciousness. On the other side, I am spit out gently. Two figures appear to my left. I recognize them instantly, both from my human existence as I traveled in Tibet, and here, all the other times I have traveled this path. They are two Taras, the Buddhist goddesses of universal compassion, one green and one white. My chosen deities, appointed to meet me here before I incarnated. I don't remember everything, but some of it is coming back to me.

White Tara stands back to my left, ever peaceful and maternal. Green Tara, the excitable one, embraces me with a youthful vigor.

"You made it!" she exclaims, as if I'd just arrived at a party. "Look at you! Oh, sister, how much you have been through. How much there still is to do!"

We look each other over. Her long, slender body is dusky olive and adorned with beautiful golden, red and green jewels, plus white bracelets and multi-stringed necklaces. I look at myself, a tall, gangly ghost of Mary Margaret, still connected to my body by a silver cord coming from my navel. How pathetic I must look to her.

"You have so much to do," she nearly sings. "We must send you on your way to see him. You don't know how boring he is, not remembering. It is like he is nothing more than a vegetable. A beautiful one, but we have plenty of beautiful gods here."

"Will you take me to Ray?" I ask, nervous. Too much Mary Margaret with me still. I want to shake it loose, be free of my human shackles. Why can't I just stay?

"With that kind of thinking, you will never pass your test!" Green Tara says, not in the least bit harsh, only speaking the truth, which tumbles out of her mouth like the gems she wears.

"Another will come to take you to him. We are just your greeters. Be assured you are doing a good job. Such harsh conditions there! Remember, if you need me, call on me for instantaneous help with lions and pride, wild elephants and delusions, forest fires and hatred, snakes and envy, robbers and fanatical views, prisons and avarice, floods and lust, demons and doubts!"

With that, she and White Tara are gone. More guides appear, perhaps a dozen, these with faces like silicone gel protruding through cellophane. They have no bodies. Again, I'm carried toward beams of light. More tunnels of living consciousness leading, I somehow know, to Divine Intelligence. To the most essential God/Goddess of Infinity. I cannot move through them, though I am seduced, wholly, toward that which cannot be resisted.

Why can't I move forward? It is this silver-blue cord, attaching me to the woman below, the woman I was. I want to tear away at it, like a trapped animal will gnaw at her own limb. It is not meant to be. I can only watch, feeling the pull, going nowhere.

So, this is the One True Journey. The only one that matters. The other journeys, with their drums and helpful drug allies, were nothing compared to this. They were navigations through my psyche, a convoluted processor that thinks too much of itself, believes itself to be real.

"Welcome," a voice says.

I remember it, from below. Wyunetta Morningstar. Great

Mother. Only bigger and brighter than I knew her.

"Black Jet Woman has allowed me the great honor of bringing you to meet your twin soul again," Great Mother says. Shivers of excitement overtake me.

She draws me sideways, as if we were on an iridescent carnival carousel moving at great speed. As we spin, I see another woman, out of the corner of my eye. With nine heads, and a golden globe behind her, she is watching me. It ought to frighten me, but I know who she is. Oya. Thanks to a young shaman in Africa, I have her power in my corner, like nine aces in the hole. We acknowledge each other as if we are two great warriors who have fought both with and against each other. The respect wells between us, a palpable field of energy, until I am pulled by the carousel to another spot outside of space and time.

At last it stops at a door made of crystal. I look in to the crack of an opening. Crystal inside and out, floor to ceiling, everywhere. Like a city. No wonder I have spent so much time trying to hear what quartz has to say. I was listening for my beloved.

At the end of the room, on a throne made of rubies, I see his hand resting on the arm of the great chair. Ah, Divinity! His, mine, ours. And freedom! Freedom at last for my true love. As if lights had been thrown on inside my head, I remember it all, every detail, every life. My Ray, the Divine Incarnation of Faith as known through Norbu. Ascended Master. I peek further and see he speaks to his subjects with wisdom and care, his eyes like honey sparkling in sunlight. It does not look boring at all to me.

"Go on," Great Mother says.

I hesitate as it all weaves together for me. To make my presence known is to cause him to remember me. To bring his attention to what is left undone, back there. To remind him of all I have done, and not done, in my own forgetfulness of who we really are. Now I am to ask him to return to where life is dim, a fraction of the pulse that is this world. To shackle him once again.

"Go on," she repeats.

How can I? How can I ask him to return to that place,

when he is already free here? When he has made it beyond the bindings of human existence? And just look at me, so ugly next to his magnificent soul.

"You must," she says, as if this is my test.

Which I now see that it is.

"It is his path. Let him see you, and he will know it," my Great Mother insists.

I hear her, and see the test for all that it is. To call him back to human existence is to know that for one to be saved, all must be saved. To save myself and our world by bringing back my whole self. But I can't. The guilt of what I put him through there hangs around my neck, a weight I cannot bear to put around his neck again. I understand that this is judging the darkness as less than the light, and so perpetuating the imbalance that is our demise. But my understanding does me no good.

My judgments keep me from moving toward him. If I don't move, I will fail this test. Which I know, having seen my own future, I already have. Where is Kenya with her magic?

"This is your destiny," Great Mother encourages again.

"I can't," I say as Ray begins to look up toward the door. I duck behind.

"Who is there?" I hear the voice of a god.

Without warning, the long cord rips at my gut, reeling me backwards with a whoosh at lightning speed, past the light, into the darkness, until again I feel a light. This one burns. The harsh sun.

I close my eyes again as I sputter and gag, water dousing my face. I turn and open my eyes to see the filthy boots of Dark Crow. He is standing over me with an empty water bottle in each hand, no doubt used to bring me around. I am confused, disoriented. Is that Eric standing beside me?

"She'll live," Dark Crow says, sounding less than enthusiastic.

Hell. I'm in hell again.

A hand beneath my own reminds me I am still touching Chief. "Chief," I say, still gagging, noticing he is not.

"Dead," Dark Crow says, not a hint of compassion or regret in his voice.

"I'm sorry, but your friend died," Eric says, as if Dark Crow had not already told me. He pats my hand, a gentle, kind gesture, but I jerk away at the stabbing pain it creates. Sunburn. How long was I gone?

Eric helps me get up. "We need to get you into the shade. You're pretty burned."

"I thought it was night," I say.

"It's barely noon," Eric relays.

Gone a whole day? Or was it even more?

"What are you doing here?" I ask.

"I was worried about you when you didn't answer the phone. This guy said he'd let me follow his truck into the canyon if I rented a four-wheeler." He gives me a look that suggests he is none too impressed with Dark Crow and points to a fancy, jet black jeep.

"I failed," I say to myself, though I am not sure what I have failed at. My head throbs, keeping me from putting the pieces together. What happened?

"You haven't failed anything," Eric says, like he has any idea. "You just passed out, or something. I'll get you out of here. I've got the jeep, and this guy can take care of the body. I'll get you to a doctor and then take you home with me. You can forget all this nonsense."

"Safe and sound," Dark Crow sneers, rolling Chief up in the sheet I carried him in.

I reach up to feel my face, sunburned, parched like the cracking earth, trying to discern what to do. I look to Dark Crow, then Eric, then Dark Crow again.

"I'm not leaving Chief," I finally say.

"Well, then," Dark Crow says, heaving the lifeless body on his back, then tossing him in the back of the truck with a thud, "you'll be goin' with me."

My stomach sinks and fear churns it around. I ignore the sensations and nod my agreement.

36

"I'm not letting you go with this guy," Eric whispers, offer-ing me a sun visor that seems to cut into my forehead as he pushes it on. "He's trouble. Come home with me. I'll take good care of you. A house and a car of your own instead of that stupid RV, anything you want. This is no life for anyone."

I feel my face again, hot and swollen. I'm hungry, weak, tired and confused. Very confused. Being taken care of sounds nice. In fact, I must have really misjudged Eric, him coming all this way to help. Maybe this is Kenya's new plan, now that the old one, whatever it was, is gone.

No, that doesn't feel right. But neither does going with Dark Crow. Didn't Chief say I was only safe so long as he was alive? Where does that leave me now? It doesn't matter. Staying with Chief's body feels like my only hope.

I look at Eric and shake my head no.

"You can't save the world," he responds, sounding exas-perated. "Don't you see that by now? Just come, save me and my world." He stops before he says he loves me, that he's always loved me, but I can see it in his face. Or hear it intu-itively.

Dark Crow snickers at Eric's plea.

"I have to go with Chief," I say.

Eric lets out an exaggerated sigh. "He's dead!"

"I know." It kills me, but I know. I turn to address Dark Crow. "Will you take him to Wyunetta's hogan?"

"She's dead, too. Yesterday," he says.

Somehow, I knew that too. Vague, partially-formed recol-lections come back to me. I saw her. Did I die? Was I supposed to do something? God, my head feels like a train wreck.

"Mary," Eric implores, irritating me, "this guy knows what

to do with the body. I'm sure there will be some kind of funeral you can go to. Come with me."

"No!" I yell at him, though he is near.

Eric looks hurt, like a wounded little boy, then pissed off. "Fine."

"I'm sorry, I have to go with Chief. I don't know why, but I have to." I can't let this all end. Not before I remember what I am supposed to do. Why do I feel like I'm late for something?

"Fine," Eric says again, in a short tone that makes it clear it is not fine at all. "Ride back in his grungy truck with a dead man. I'm going home to a gin and tonic and a hundred cable channels. You can spend eternity trying to save a world the rest of us are happy as clams in."

For a moment, it's tempting. A gin and tonic, a nice comfy leather couch, mind-numbing television.

"Just another prison," I say softly, tossing the visor away from me. Yet something about a prison rings a bell. I remember a crystal room and a god in it. The idea sends me off, wondering, as the world spins about me.

"Your choice, Mary," Eric says a few moments later from his driver's seat, extending the invitation one more time.

I shake my head. He leaves me to my fate with a look that says I'm a fool. Perhaps I am. I get in Dark Crow's truck, weak and trembling. As before, we ride in silence, my driver looking at me like I'm dirt. I remember this part from the ride in. Didn't Wyunetta say not to go with him again? But what choice do I have?

I trace the last few days in my mind, putting the puzzle together. It starts to form. The journeys. A plan. A test. I died. Why does being alive feel like I failed? Can I do anything now? Know what you know, Chief taught. You have all the answers inside you. Easier said than done when even the questions are as evasive as drops of oil in a bowl of water.

"Where are we going?" I ask as we turn off the main canyon path. My gift of seeing does not serve me well at the moment. I remember seeing the fist shattering a cheek. I hear thoughts, like words from a distance, in Dark Crow's voice. Something about having a little fun, now that Chief is out of the way.

"I have some friends back here, need to know about Chief," he lies.

I hate him for it. For his disrespect of Chief. My heart is racing. This is not good.

Dark Crow looks at me and chuckles. I look out the window and remember the bird, but can't find it. That's right, I healed myself of that escapism. But for what? To live what is coming full force?

"Go into the pain," I remember someone saying. Where was that? Georgia?

Damn it, I need to think. My tongue starts to flap in my mouth. I hear it say it doesn't want me to swear.

Okay, I'm going out of my mind.

He turns sharply into an outlet and throws the gear into park. No hogans in sight. Nothin'.

Oh yes, I remember Nothin'.

Dark Crow pulls his knife, gleaming in the sunlight, and turns toward me, as though we were going to have a nice conversation. "So, you gonna lift your skirt or do I get the pleasure of rippin' it off?"

I can't breathe, let alone talk.

"I've only done this twice before," Dark Crows admits freely, "but I never forget that look in the eyes afterwards. Just Nothin' left." He lunges at me quickly, snapping his teeth. "I'm gonna eat your power, then I'll be The One."

I freeze.

He lifts my skirt, his knife nicking my thigh, while his other hand loosens his belt. His cock flies free, hard and eager, already glistening with anticipation. I reach behind me to find the door handle.

"Don't even fuckin' think about it," he growls, his face contorted in disgust, and raises his empty fist.

Time stops.

I've seen this scene. Been here before.

Like magic, with all the time in the world, I step outside of myself. There was something here, I think, fully calm, patient for it to come to me.

Oh, yes. A seed. A message. I'll just allow it. It will come.

I hear my own voice in my ear. "Remember who you are."

It all clicks. Everything. The puzzle back intact, just like that. I've seen this future in order to have the power to change it.

"You can't have me ever again!" I scream into the frozen moment.

Without warning I am back in my body, his fist only inches from my face. I turn my head as the fist just grazes my ear.

Like magic, I see everything so clearly. A full ashtray, a lone cigarette still lit. In a split second I rip the metal container from its perch, smashing the filth into Dark Crow's face. Ash flies, a distraction. I use my precious seconds to grab the door and fall out of it.

"Fuckin' bitch!" he screams. "Now I'm gonna cut you in a thousand pieces."

I stumble out of the truck, looking for something, anything, to buy me time. My nemesis moves out my door behind me, then stops abruptly. I turn to see what has stopped him, unable to fathom what is before me.

Puck, with a rifle nearly as big as himself, pointed at Dark Crow.

"No, Puck!" I yell, diving, despite myself, to push my enemy out of the line of fire. Not to save Dark Crow, but Puck's sweet innocence.

Dark Crow lunges toward Puck and a shot goes off.

A window shatters, blood and body splatters.

Puck is thrown back several feet.

Dark Crow's mutilated dead weight slowly edges its way down the passenger door his own body has rammed shut, his knife still clutched in his hand.

I look at myself—blood and plasma, chunks of skin and scalped hair splattered on me, mixing with cigarette ash, like a sick work of art. Turning, I see a the essence of a ghost rise up out of a terrified Puck, just as my own did during my journeys. When, if ever, he will be able to come back and retrieve this piece of his soul?

I run to him, pull him to me, try to grab at his ghost, but it is too late. Together, we are baptized in darkness, hell on our heels.

His head tucked under my chin, a silent scream contorts

my mouth. Puck wraps his arms around my waist, holding on tight. For him, I attempt to gather myself together, swallowing the emotion.

We sit in eerie silence until Puck slowly points in the direction of the dead body. Already the vultures are circling above. But it is Dark Crow himself, his shadow of a ghost, who has started eating his own mangled form.

"Can you see that?" I ask Puck, though he is the one who has pointed it out to me.

He nods, afraid.

"Me too."

Here, in this alcove, everything is alive. Other ghosts come swooping in, joining the feast. A horror film in front of our eyes.

"We have to get out of here," I say quietly, as if the ghosts might hear and turn to begin eating us. I grab his hand and slowly move to the driver's door of the truck. I wipe off the broken bits of glass and cigarette butts left on the seat, slicing my hands, getting Dark Crow's filthy ashes in my bloodstream. It could have been worse. Maybe.

When the seat is free of glass, Puck gets in, sliding across the seat's big rip.

One nightmare over. A new one begun.

37

I turn the key, still in the ignition. A shiver runs up my spine and a cold feeling overtakes me. Is it Dark Crow's ghost? Has he noticed our escape? Or is it only a bogeyman? More of my wild imagination?

I peel out, leaving Dark Crow's body to fall away from the truck, not brave enough to look back. I trace the wheel tracks backwards toward the main canyon and stop. Which way to go?

Think, Mary, think.

Logic takes hold. A dead man wrapped in a sheet lies in the back of the truck. Another is shot to hell behind us. There will be police. Questions. The real world.

I look at Puck, still silent, eyes glazed, lost in this nightmare. When they come for us, he will be taken away from me. If he cries to me for comfort, it will not be allowed. There will be vultures there, too, picking at the evil. Puck will see them. I will see them. I could play the game, probably, and stay silent. He won't be able to. He'll freak out. They will assume he is insane. Take him God knows where. I don't need any psychic gifts to see all of that.

Yet to see is to have the opportunity to change what I see, I remind myself yet again. I move my eyes to examine his body, then mine. I am filthy with blood, body tissue and hair, even bits of black T-shirt plastered across me. Puck seems not to have noticed, yet, that it has also rubbed off on him. We need to wash.

The sacred waterfall.

I hear the words as if spoken aloud. Whose voice? Mine? I don't know, but the waterfall is the answer. There will come a time when all is beyond my control, when the nightmare will have a life of its own. But for now, I can walk with my young friend, give us both time to calm down, then clean up in the stream. I'll make up some story about the sacred waterfall cleansing us. Maybe it will even be true. This, at the least, I can do for my little savior.

I turn east towards the camp I knew I would see again, praying we meet up with no tours and no natives. I imagine ourselves invisible, a meager attempt at shapeshifting a beat-up truck, woman and child. The terrain is difficult to navigate, unaccustomed as I am to driving on the sandy canyon floor. We bounce and bump, saying not a word. I apologize to Chief, in the back, knowing first-hand how hard that waffled flatbed is. Even if he is not with us, his remains deserve tenderness.

I begin to cry silent tears.

Oh, Chief! How could you have gone so soon? Why did you trust me? How could you believe I was even remotely ready? Look, look at what has happened to us. Chief is silent, of course. As is Puck, staring out the window, as if at Nothin', remembering something he may not recover from. I scoot him toward me. However hellish this has been, I'm the adult.

"It's gonna be okay, honey," I say, putting my arm around him. Even if it is not. Even if it will never be okay again.

He pulls away to look me in the eyes, his own clouded and confused, his little forehead wrinkled with worry. "I had to save you," he whispers hoarsely, sorrow filling each word to overflowing. At least he's talking again.

"You did, baby," I say, wondering for the first time how that could be. How had he known I was there? What made him come, right then, and with a gun as big as himself? Did Kenya send angels? Could that mean there is still a way? I curse myself for having hope, yet remember who I am. It saved me once.

"Why do we have to kill?'" he asks.

Like I know such a thing? Like I know anything at all?

I suppose I ought to. After all, I've even seen the True Way, the Other Side. Still, I have no answers for this. Little Puck—my Hannah, my Lilly—is looking to me to have an answer. But I don't. I pull him tighter, caress his forehead with my free hand.

No answers, but I can hold him. Maybe that is all any of us can do, all the answer there is. To comfort each other through the hell of this existence. I look out the back window to the lifeless form behind.

What now, my Chief? Now that I have not only failed to save myself, and any part of my world, but taken down an innocent with me? I let out a heavy breath and see my hand shaking on the wheel. I hear no reply.

We drive in silence until Spider Rock appears. I will have to leave Chief in the truck. I hide the vehicle as well as I can, between a heavy clustering of trees. They will lend their camouflage enough to fool those who are not looking. It is only a matter of time, which has never been so acutely real to me as it is now.

I lead Puck to the trail he knows better than I, holding his little boy brown hand in my thin, trembling, sun-burned one. He asks no questions. Which is good, because I have no answers.

Think, Mary. Think.

An old voice. One that used to believe thinking could make a difference. But my brain is shot. Too many journeys, too much tragedy. One foot in front of the other is all I can muster.

The animals have abandoned us, I notice. The honor they bestowed upon Chief in his final walk is not offered to a young killer and his white woman caretaker.

"Stop!" I say, evenly but firmly, squeezing Puck's hand hard. He sees it, too. A rattler. We stand unmoving, letting it consider us.

Moments pass. More. The rattle is deafening.

Remembering, I pray to Green Tara. Didn't she say she offers protection from lions and pride, wild elephants and more? I think snakes were in there somewhere. Immediate help, she promised.

Stunned, I see the rattler move on for no reason. Without discussion, my little companion and I resume walking.

So, I was wrong. The animal kingdom has not abandoned us. But what is it offering? A warning? A chance in the lottery of life and death? Or change, as Chief had said on one of my earlier trips to the waterfall?

I can almost hear his voice. "If you come across a rattler, it will be a good sign."

A good sign. We need that. But what can I change now?

China.

The word comes from the same voice that directed me here, toward the waterfall. I cannot say if I have heard it with my ears, in actuality, but I did hear it.

China? I ask, silently.

China.

I hear the word, plain as day.

Puck, if he has heard, says nothing.

But how? I've no drummer. No plant medicine.

I hear nothing in reply. Then, at last.

Your heartbeat is a drum.

I wonder, can I do it? Can I journey to the beat of my own heart? No Chief. No instrument. No smoking with sage. No spirit honoring ceremony. Just me, out here, as I walk.

Everything you need is inside of you.

Is this Chief's voice? No.

Your own.

Mine? Me, telling me what to do? That's just my imagination, then. I can't trust that.

I hear no reply.

So, this is the crux of it. To leap yet again into the void, trusting only the sound of my own voice. One that tells me, in the fragile condition I am already in, to return to China, where insanity has been waiting for centuries. Didn't we kill Dark Crow? Isn't that over?

No.

But I don't know what to do when I get there.

You will.

At least a mile has passed without a word from Puck. Shock, no doubt. Would he notice me mentally check out for an internal journey? Probably not.

I consider my options and realize I have none. But I suppose if I believe I can pull a miracle out of a waterless sacred waterfall, it's no great leap to listen to the strange voice in my head telling me to do the one thing I failed to do with

Chief as my guide. What can it hurt to try?

I slow my breath, listen for my heart, making my footsteps as even as I can. Still, I can't hear. With my free hand, I put it on my neck, find my pulse. It helps. I find it, feel it. I soften my eyes, go in. Deeper. Breathe. Deeper. Slow.

Allow.

Thump, thump, thump....

Allow.

I purposefully imagine the tree roots, going down. I move and sway, finding myself rocking back and forth slightly, even as I walk, hearing the drum of my own heart.

"Help me Chief," I mouth to the sky, making no sound so as not to disturb Puck. "Help me walk between the drumbeats."

38

Past the tree roots, I finally see what I need to see. The ocean with her backwards waves. I make myself smell the moist salt air, hear seagulls. I'm going. Letting myself go. Farther and farther, until Hangchow comes into view. The stench rises. Rotting bodies, urine and feces.

I'm here, in the cell, early in my night alone with Ray. My soul has just split, its ghost hovering in the corner. It is an ugly coward, evil in its small, arrogant, selfish ways.

I look closer. So this is me?

"This is all of us," Lion says, surprising me with her presence. "Darkness and light, capable of evil, capable of love. When you own what you are capable of, you no longer need another to bring it to light—another who will make choices against your truest wish. When you hold all things possible, you hold the power to choose."

"I know I gave that power to Dark Crow. I've seen what he does with it, again and again. I want my power back."

"Then you must change what happened here," Lion says.

"How can I? You can't change the past."

"You can. The past is no more real than the future, remember. Here, in the dreaming body of non-ordinary reality, you can change anything you want. Change it as you wish here, the effects will show up, there."

I see that Ray has noticed me.

"So it is all up to me? Whatever I dream becomes reality?"

"No, he must play his role and make his own choices. You must consider what he wishes, too."

That seems fair enough. Finding a courage born of desperation, I lie my soul atop the guard I once was, immediately nauseated. As the guard, I approach Ray, my prisoner.

"Don't worry, I won't hurt you," I say.

Ray says nothing, looking wary, curling against a wall. A reasonable response. What am I to say? What can I say? What can I do?

Tell him what you feel.

My inner voice, here, too. Good. I try to imagine Ray's position.

"I want you to understand," I begin, then hesitate. We are speaking without words. It takes some adjustment. "I don't want to hurt you anymore."

"I don't want to be hurt," Ray replies.

"I will let you go, if you want, but there are dangers in that. If I do, they will hunt you and find you. It will be worse when you return, and then you will surely die. If I do not continue to hurt you at least some, they will notice. They will see I am too slack, and someone else will harm you more than I would. You will surely die that way, too."

Ray softens his back from the wall and looks into my eyes. His broken body still shakes with fear—a learned response I cannot blame him for. "I know you do this out of care for me. That is why I sing for you."

My guard's hardened heart melts at his words. "For me? I imagined you must have been singing for God."

Ray smiles—the first I have seen as his tormentor. My melting heart rips and tears in all directions.

"To find care like yours in a hell such as this makes me believe there must be a God."

I fall to one knee, reach for his hand and press it to my heart. "Forgive me, please. Tell me what to do. Whatever you say, I will do it."

His voice rings calm and clear. "I forgive you. Will you sing me a song this time?"

I nod.

"Then," he adds, "take your baton and strike me once, here." He points to his jugular, the very place I hold my fingers to my neck, up there, as Mary Margaret, in the canyon.

"I can't!" I say.

"God will find me where your care leaves me."

I pull my soul away, unable to contain my tears. "Lion,

Lion, how can I do this? How can I kill the one I love? How?"

"Take back the shadow of your soul," Lion says firmly, "the fragment over there in the corner. In doing so, you will once again be capable of anything."

"I don't want to be capable of that!"

"Then you will still need a shadow to do it for you. Dark Crow will ever be willing. Remember, wholeness is darkness and light, so that even death can be chosen, in the name of love."

I look to the soul fragment, that me which cannot be me, but is. It snickers, jeers in silence, as if daring me. Surely, I am not capable of what Ray asks without this part of my soul returned.

I consider for what feels like an eternity.

"Come back," I finally force myself to say. My dark, fragmented soul needs no encouragement. Power surges through me as I become finally, fully whole.

Stronger than I have ever been, in a way I never dreamed, I lay my soul over that of the guard again. Together we stand, and I gather my weapon.

A song chokes out of me as the guard, a song of bittersweet parting. It seems to calm Ray, please him even, as he lives out his stay of execution.

The song over, with one swift blow, I take his life.

Tripping on a log, up there as Mary Margaret, I am brought back to reality in one swift fall. Puck stumbles too, still holding my hand. I grab him and hug him, never wanting to let go. Good God, have I only made things worse? Taken back my own evil? Killed the one I love with my own hands? I feel it, surging through me. Power. Good or bad, I don't know.

Just power.

Well, I may need it in the days ahead.

I look up to see we have arrived at Chief's homestead, neatly packed away, as if we were never here. But we were. These journeys may be all imagination, but Chief did live. He did believe in it all. Now I must as well.

The waterfall is not far.

"Let's go wash in the stream by the sacred waterfall," I say to Puck, trying to sound optimistic. He looks at himself, and for the first time notices the horror we need washing from. He shrieks, tears off his shirt and takes off running toward the creek. I am still spent from my journeys and weak from no food. I stumble after him, calling for him to wait, promising it will be okay, forcing myself to be the Hope that I am.

We reach the stream, now a mere trickle. Not enough to drink from, let alone bathe in. It angers me. Deeply. Something new in me stirs, a darkness beyond the pent-up anger Chief worked so hard to help me lance. My soul retrieval worked. I am darkness and light, the polarity of all that is within me. The animal has been let back in, yet it is still far from tame. God help us all.

The darkness grows, powerful.

"Is a little water so much to ask?" I yell into the canyon.

The birds quiet, then start again. As if nothing has happened. As if the world were not chaos. As if my beautiful Puck did not need to be cleansed.

He looks at me, eyes huge, brow furrowed, about to jump out of his own skin.

Then he looks past me, eyes bulging.

"Angels," he says. "Do you see them, Mary? Do you see them?"

I look behind me, expecting to see a legion of winged helpers, bringing the miracle Puck deserves. After all, I braved China for just such help. I see only more canyon, more pinion trees, more dirt. Still, and ever, I am on my own.

"Do you see them?" he asks.

I cannot and will not lie to him. "No Puck, but that does not mean they aren't there. I'm not so good at seeing a lot of the time."

My own lack of sight angers me further. How often I have weakened, failed to save myself and the world I love. It grows, like a thunder from the distance, until it comes full force, cracking in my face.

Thunder. Yes, that is it! Thunder. Lightning.

Oya.

"Stand back, Puck," I say, willing myself to believe, or at least dream.

Puck examines my face. "Don't go without me," he pleads.

"I don't know if this will work," I admit. I do know it is dangerous, and even if it does work, it may only cause more harm.

Puck falls to his knees, grabs my legs, holding tight. "I know where you're going. Chief told me. To a new place. A new life. I want to go, too. I've dreamed of it, just like you said. Don't leave me, Mommy. Please don't leave me."

Mommy? Is that what he said? Or was it Mary? Even if I heard him wrong, I know that is my role. At least in this moment.

"I'll never leave you, Puck," I promise. I move to stand where the waterfall, were it falling, would meet the canyon. Let all hell break loose if it will. I'm dreaming a new dream. Puck is included. "Hold on, no matter what, okay?"

He nods into my legs.

I stand my feet a little wider apart, planting them firmly.

"Oya," I yell, a call that comes from the depths of my anger, deeper than I knew I could go. From beyond the darkness and the light.

Nothing but a faint echo returns.

"Oya," I raise my volume. "Let the sacred waters flow!"

Nothing but a sun that burns, though the birds stay quiet this time.

Do not call to the Oya out there. She is not out there. She is within.

In the bush, I see a rustle, something golden amid the foliage.

"A lion," Puck whispers in awe.

"Good," I say, willing myself to believe.

I call upon all the animals, their manna, as I once did in Hawaii.

"Oya!" I yell, this time into myself, into the worlds within worlds that I am, dreaming that Chief's dream lives in me.

In the distance, out there, a slight rumble. Then another, and another. Clouds form. White, then gray, then dark, rolling toward us, tumbling over each other, eager.

For a brief moment, sunlight and darkness share the same space, day dances with night. The canyon walls respond, as if an artist has thrown an impossible wash of soft violet and magenta at them, letting the rocks cry out, not in words, but watercolors. I have seen the desert paint itself like this before. This time, though, it feels like a private show, created just for us. Even so, I will not stop, or say "good enough." Beauty alone is not enough. Not anymore.

"Oooooyyyyaaaaa!" It is a powerful, guttural growl, a lion in my throat. I dream of Ray, returning to be what the world needs and I alone cannot provide.

The rain begins light, then heavy, until sheets roll over us. Soon, the sacred waterfall begins, cascading down in ribbons. Puck and I stand at the edge as cool, clean water washes away the Dark Crow.

Even now, with this great grace, I do not stop. I want more. I want the dream.

"Ooooyyaaaa.....Oooooyyyaaaaa.....Ooooooyyyyaaaaaa...."

It becomes a chant as the thunder bellows, drowning me out.

The lightning flashes, distant.

Then not so distant.

The next one, I know that I know, comes for us.

I see it from miles away, a jagged flash of power I have invoked and stand ready to be responsible for.

"Ooooooyyyyy............." The flash pierces my left shoulder, lighting me through, extending to the brave little boy trembling at my feet.

Within the flash, a pair of golden-brown eyes peer directly into my own. In those eyes, I again know what I know.

Ray has seen me.

The God I am has remembered.

39

"What time is it?" I ask, sitting straight up in bed.

Ray puts down his book to reach and turn the clock toward him. "Only eleven-thirty," he says. "You okay?"

I feel myself, touching a hand to my left shoulder, finding it intact. Suddenly, my stomach revolts, sending me to the toilet.

"You're not pregnant again, are you?" he asks from the other room, quiet enough to not wake the kids.

The kids? The thoughts compute easily, but also seem foreign to me. I press my hot head against the cool toilet bowl. "I think it was the fish," I return.

"Could be," Ray agrees, not sounding convinced, making his way to the bathroom. He wets a rag in the sink and presses it against my forehead. My beloved Ray, always good when the chips are down.

Ray?

I look at him, as if it were the first time.

Tall, black hair, barrel chest, brown eyes with golden flecks that dance when he smiles. Best looking Navajo I ever met. Wisest, too.

"Chief had the fish, too," he says. "She was fine when I tucked her in."

It all hits me. Chief. Here? A she? The next great teacher is a she?

Of course. Chief Of No Tribe. Our daughter was so dubbed by Jimmy Two Feathers, a member of Ray's clan, for her amazing wisdom, which she started touting at the ripe age of two. Now she is seven, just like the older Chief had dreamed.

Two lifetimes of memories come together like two decks of cards shuffled into one. A perfect, seamless dovetail that allows me to remember Chief, the soul I knew back there, in the canyon. And my daughter, the same soul who nursed at my breast. Just as it was dreamed.

"Didn't Puck have some fish, too?" he asks, taking the cloth, rinsing it out in cool water and offering it to me again.

Puck! Amazing Puck! My five-year-old boy. Biggest hockey fan you've ever seen.

"He made it," I say aloud.

"Made what?"

I don't answer, only move from the toilet bowl back to the bed, feeling shaky.

"Mommy," Puck says, rubbing his eyes, standing at the door.

"Baby, what are you doing up?" I ask.

Oh, Puck! Same little body, similar features. And why not? He is half Navajo. And not a switch mark on him.

"Hey, little man, you're not feeling sick are you?" Ray asks.

Little man. A surge of love rises in me for my husband of nine years, familiar and yet new. Faith incarnate, just a man, a good daddy, a loving husband. We have our troubles, but no more than any other happily married couple.

"Chief had another dream," Puck says. Behind him, Chief appears, a dark-haired goddess. Eyes so blue, miraculous replicas of mine, and cheeks fair. A cherub of the highest order. But thin, always too thin.

"Really? Tell us," Ray says, scooting over to make room for them both.

Ah, yes. The dreams. Now it makes sense. Chief is a tough one to get to sleep, and always looks like her eyes are open even in the middle of the night. Her dreams, more like visions, have become a constant source of amazement. Though I have often downplayed them, Ray always takes them seriously. After all, he's the shaman of the family. I'm just a logical, semi-uptight housewife, struggling to get something written on my doctoral dissertation.

"What happened this time, sweetie?" I ask.

"Daddy was a god," she begins.

"Damn, I like this dream!" Ray says with a grin.

"Don't swear," I say out of habit. Realizing the shift, from me swearing to Ray, I laugh so hard I almost fall out of bed. Chief looks at me with a twinkle in her eyes. Could she know? Could it really be true? Did she plan out even this little detail? Or am I going nuts?

"Hey!" Puck interjects in his usual explosive style, "I saw angels. Real angels, with white wings and tons of feathers and they flew around like it wasn't hard at all and nobody even could see them but me because I am an angel or I was before this lifetime when...."

"Angels? You mean in Chief's dream?" Ray interrupts, which is really the only thing you can do when Puck gets rolling. At least no one in this family has ever told him he bores us to death.

"No," he says in all seriousness, obviously unaware of where we have just come from. "Real angels. I was asleep, and then I woke up and I saw them in my room and they said that Chief was a great messenger come to help save the world." He sticks his chest out and beams, ever in love with his big sister.

"Is that right?" I ask, looking to my daughter. "What do you think of that, Chief?"

"What if it's dangerous?" she asks, looking coy.

I know my daughter. This question is not coming from her own fear, but her knowledge of mine. I'm forever anxious about what bad things could happen, telling her to be careful. My shrink suggests it has come from losing Hannah the way I did. I wonder now, knowing what I know, if I'll be able to ease up a bit. Maybe, but until I get this figured out a little more, I'd best stick to how I would respond as her mother.

"Well, then, you will have to be careful," I tell her.

She looks at me, deadpan. "What if I can't?"

I feel a pang in my heart, a tearing. What does she know of this Great Teacher business that I do not? I answer with a certainty I do not feel. "Then you will have to be brave and strong."

Chief smiles. "I can do that, Mommy. I know I can."

"I know you can too, sweetie," I say.

"Okay, enough of this," Ray insists in his authoritative, daddy-means-business voice, though it scares none of us. "It's late. We can hear all about it tomorrow. Mommy's not feeling well, and we all have a big day ahead of us."

Without further prodding, they race off.

Amazing.

"I'm feeling better now," I say, though it is only beginning to be true. "I think I'll go tuck them in again. You'll be up when I get back?"

"I'll be here," he says, lifting his book.

I walk down the hall, marveling at the pictures that hang as proof of years that did not exist. I touch them, just to be sure. They are as real as it gets. So maybe my life as a bookmobile driver was just a dream. I fade in and out of certainty, as if I'm still not quite awake.

Chief is waiting for me in the hall. "I did good, didn't I, Sweet Mary?"

Sweet Mary?

I look at her intently. Does she know? Shoot, do I know?

"You head on in to bed. I'll be in to talk in just a minute," I promise, then turn into Puck's room.

Tucking him in, I realize that, whoever he is, and whoever he has been in whatever dreams I have dreamed and realities I have lived, he is my little boy now. All mine, to love and protect. There are no beatings to remember, no negligent parents, no murders. Just the task of being a boy, going to sleep in my house, on the bed I have made for him. I pull the comforter up to his chin and caress his brow.

"I really did see angels," he assures me, yawning.

"I believe you," I reply, knowing that it is the first time I really do.

I hum to him, sitting on the edge of the bed, the way he likes. Soon enough, he is fast asleep. "Goodnight my Hannah, my Lilly," I whisper, kissing him, knowing what I have always known but never been able to feel so fully—that I am the luckiest woman in the world.

Taking a breath of intention, I move to Chief's room. She has her rotating lamp on, turning stars on the ceiling. She has slept with this nightlight since she was a baby, hearing her Daddy's stories of how the stars hold the sky together.

"Can we rock?" she asks me, already moving toward our special chair. She knows I cannot refuse this, however big she gets. We snuggle in, her head tucked into my shoulder. I revel in it, as though it were the first time. Maybe it is.

"Tell me more about your dream," I request, matching my voice to the magical night hour.

"You know it was not a dream, Sweet Mary. Know what you know."

"You...you know about all of this? This dream within a dream?"

"Of course. Love *is* consciousness."

"Big ideas for a little girl. Or am I the little girl, and you've only been pretending all these years? Years that didn't exist?"

"We did it," young Chief replies, as if that says it all.

"And you're a girl! I didn't expect that."

"The feminine has been lost for too long. That is the beginning of my message."

Amazing.

"So now what, my wise messenger?"

"I will remember, but you will forget. You still have things to learn."

"I'm quite sure of that," I say, inhaling the scent of little girl and baby shampoo, taking it down to the tips of my toes. "You will be safe, won't you?"

"Life is not safe," she reminds me. "But this life is not all there is. You have learned that."

"I hope, once I forget, that I learn it again soon."

Chief sits up and pulls back to look at me. "If that is your dream, why don't you plant a seed in your future?"

The idea instantly grabs me. "What do you suggest?"

"One more journey," she replies, as if it has been an idea of hers all along. "Tomorrow. I've been taking on some of your tummy upset since you woke up, so it won't be a lie if I have to stay home from school tomorrow. I can drum for you."

"The drum! That's right!" The drum, addressed to me as Mary Margaret Begaye at our house on Juniper Street in Scottsdale! It arrived yesterday from Wyunetta. "Great Mother," as we all call her. She has taken a real liking to me even though I am a white woman, and always insists I stay for a meal. Jimmy, who was like a big brother to Ray while growing up, was more wary. But he finally came around.

"She died," Chief says gently, as if unsure how I will take it. "You'll learn about it tomorrow."

"Yes. I saw her in the other world." The other world I am about to forget. I wonder how much of a seed I can plant. "Okay, tomorrow we journey."

Chief nuzzles against me again.

"Do you know how I know that you and I are truly one?" I ask, soft as a lullaby.

"Hmmm?"

"Because this life, this dream you have dreamed for us, is exactly as I would have dreamed it. Exactly."

"I know," she replies, sounding unusually tired.

Yeah, I know you know.

We rock until at last she sleeps, open-mouthed, innocent. For the first time in her seven years, it appears to me a deep and sound resting.

"It's about time," I whisper into her hair, sealing her sleep with a kiss.

I tuck her in and make my way to my beloved. Seeing with two sets of eyes, I realize there are some changes I want to make with him. Changes in the way I have done things, the fears I have allowed to limit me. Some Nothin's that need attending to, now that I have the power, and while I have consciousness to dream anew.

Through the door, I see him, propped up by half a dozen pillows, his reading glasses perched on his nose. Drop dead sexy. That was never the problem between us. It's always been me. Just me. Now, with Faith at my side, I claim the self-healing I created through my journeys. Like wind in my sails, I can feel the natural strength that has always been mine for the taking.

"What are you reading this time?" I ask Ray, scared to move toward him, knowing how crazy that is, after all these years.

"The Tao," he replies. "Says here you can let go and get whatever you want."

I laugh, wondering if the book somehow made it into my dreams. I've never heard of it here, in this life, before right now. "Sounds good, though not so easy for a girl like me."

"Some of us are strung a little tighter than others," he says with a knowing smile. He's always taken my being so wound up with a grain of salt.

"I had a dream, too," I blurt out.

"You? Dream? That's new."

I nod. "It was a lot like Chief's. A lot."

"Seriously?" He is intrigued, never doubting.

"I think it had to do with that statue you ordered when you were in Africa."

"The Oya? You think this was a shamanic dream?" He sounds so excited.

"Yeah, maybe. The statue has been...kind of...I don't know...talking to me. Anyway, I read up on her when I took the kids to story hour today. She's a goddess of weather. Stormy weather and tumultuous change."

"We can get rid of her if you want," he offers.

"No. It's just that...." Tears begin to fall.

"Honey," he says, moving toward me. I stop him with a hand. He is accustomed to this gesture. I use it all too often, whenever I feel vulnerable. That is what is going to change. Me, stopping my own life, because I am afraid to feel.

"Just let me get through this," I say. "You know I'm a bit skeptical of anything supposedly divine."

"An understatement," he interjects with a laugh.

"Even so, before I went to bed, I told this Oya if there was any chance she had some power to do something with me...with my limitations...that...well, I wanted a change."

I take a deep breath. "Then I went to bed early, because I was so tired, and I had this dream that Oya was in. And now I realize why things are the way they are, and how closed I have been, always logical, not feeling, afraid of getting too close to you, of really having you, because I might lose you."

"Mary, honey, you are not going to lose me, ever. You are the love of my life."

His words are a sacred waterfall all to themselves. Enough to inspire me, and move me where I need to be.

"Wait here," I say, heading in to the bathroom. I turn back, "Don't go to sleep, okay?"

"Not for a million dollars."

Inside, with the door closed, I splash water on my face,

brush my teeth and hair, and go rummaging through the walk-in closet. I know it is here somewhere.

There it is. I pull out the nightgown he gave me more than a year ago. A leopard print, so exotic I just blushed and stuck it away. I've promised myself, again and again, I would wear it for him. I just could not get up the courage.

"It's not a lion," I whisper to myself, "but it will have to do."

It falls silky over my shoulders, reminding me of how the water felt against my naked skin in Hawaii. The sensual beauty of my soul returned, I can see myself wearing it for him now. Still scared, but strong enough to push past it.

I look at my body, a little more worn for the wear of two births, but still pretty much me. Opening the door, I stand in it, trembling. Ray looks up, his eyes widening as he pulls off his glasses.

"I want to make love like it's the first time," I say, knowing how dumb that sounds. But it is the first time. Even if he doesn't know it, I want him to feel it too.

"Damn," he says, "this Tao stuff really works."

40

Chief drums eloquently, though in this life I know it is new to her. I go down, deep and fast. Lion appears at my side, looking like a proud Mama herself. Proud of me. I can't help but grin sheepishly. In no time, we pass the forest where the animals and spirit beings appear, bowing to me. This time I am not self-conscious. I know I have done well. Maybe not perfect, but I am human after all.

Kenya swings open her door wide and we embrace like long-lost sisters. A far cry from our first encounter, with me extending myself no further than a cautious handshake.

"Thank you," I whisper, "thank you so much."

She gives a deep squeeze, steps back and takes my hand. "Just following orders. Here for a transfer request?" She smiles wide, so that I know she is teasing.

"No," I say. "My life is perfect. Better than I dreamed. Ray drives me nuts sometimes, and the kids can push my buttons, and my incomplete dissertation is still killing me. But I have all I ever wanted."

She laughs, full and hearty. "You've come a long way," she says, walking me into her cave and sitting me down. "I'll make tea."

I watch her hips sway in that purely feminine way, her bangles tinkling as she moves. I had a little of that in me, last night. Ray sure noticed. I made sure neither of us slept.

"Chief sends her...his...whatever...Chief sends love."

She turns and smiles. "An amazing soul."

I nod, watching her take out three cups.

"We're expecting company," she says to my unasked question.

"Anyone I know?" I ask. "I wouldn't mind seeing Wyunetta

Morningstar."

"She's already preparing to incarnate again," Kenya says with a mischievous look, and I realize she's a bubble ready to burst.

I catch her meaning on the air. I know what I know.

"So, I am pregnant again." I hold my stomach, feeling life even before it can be felt, knowing the mother who loved me, pounded on the Divine's door for me, will now be mine to nurture.

"It's all so hard to believe. And I'm not even sure what happened. How did Ray finally see me?"

"Wyunetta again. She banged on his door for a while. He didn't believe her, of course. Like you, in a state of hopelessness, had to choose hope, so he in faithlessness had to choose faith. She spoke to him, he stepped into the void, and there you were."

"What did she say?"

"I'm not sure I remember, exactly," she replies, knowing I know better than that, "but I'm pretty sure I recall the words 'damn fool' in there somewhere."

I laugh. That could refer to either one of us.

The doorbell sounds. Kenya moves to answer it. In the doorway, a short, solid, dark-haired woman appears. I stand to greet her as our hostess ushers her in.

"Mary," she introduces, "meet Robin, your seed."

"You know about that?" I ask Kenya, then realize how silly a question it is. We all laugh.

I look at Kenya's new guest, wondering what kind of seed she is to be. She only returns the questioning look, as though she has no idea either. We lock eyes, and an affinity grows. Somewhere, somehow, we have known each other. Or will in the future.

Kenya motions us to sit. We sink into the cushions. "Robin has been told for years that she has a special mission."

"Not that anyone will tell me what it is," Robin says good-naturedly.

"I know that tune," I say, feeling at ease with these two. Like old, old friends.

"Worry not, ladies, all will be revealed," Kenya says, obviously pleased with her secret.

Robin and I look to her eagerly.

"Well," she begins, "Robin is a writer. A storyteller. She's been asking about what Divine Guidance would have her write next."

"For about three years, now," Robin interjects with good humor. "Kenya just keeps saying 'wait, wait'."

"Of course I couldn't say a word," our hostess replies, looking positively gleeful, like a woman whose grand party is finally coming together.

"What does this have to do with me?" I ask.

"Your story, Mary. It is to be your seed. Tell it to Robin, now, while you remember. She'll have to change all the details, of course, so you don't recognize yourself. But someday, when the time is just right—you'll have to leave that to me—I'll find a way to get the story into your hands. You will again learn the very lessons you were taught in the canyon, never knowing it is all about you."

I can see it. A book, dropping mysteriously from a shelf, or being passed on through a friend, or waiting for me in an airplane seat where someone "accidentally" left it behind. I read it and relearn what I am about to forget. I might even wonder if it could be about me after all.

"Perfect," I say.

"It's an amazing story," Kenya says to Robin.

They both look at me expectantly. I start talking, recounting all I can remember, from the selenite at Jimmy's shop right up to the part where I remember that Puck never seems to live past childhood.

Panic strikes mid-sentence.

"Kenya," I plead, "do I have to worry? Will I lose him? My little boy?" At this moment, I am pure mother, knowing the risk that every mother takes, the risk of loss. "Oh, Kenya, he's my son. I can't lose him again."

Kenya smiles, but the sadness is evident on her face.

I race through my memories, trying to find a trace of my nemesis here, in this current reality. "I haven't seen Dark Crow once in this new life," I say. "Is he really dead? Are we really free?"

Even as I say this, I remind myself that tragedy can come through many doors. After all, I lost Hannah, long before I met Dark Crow.

"Puck is not just any child," Kenya explains gently.

"He's not?" I ask, hopeful.

"No," she replies. "He is a Divine Incarnation of Innocence, born in the angelic realms. As a service to mankind, to show how beautiful life can be, he incarnates again and again, playing the same role. Each time we wait to see if the world is changed enough for pure innocence to finally live past childhood. It is a big dream, but that is part of why Norbu is here. Yet for such a great dream, we must all dream it together."

I nod, tears threatening me.

I'm dreaming, Puck. I'm dreaming.

Even as I do, I notice something. Something strange in the air. Kenya is not telling me everything.

"What is it?" I ask, sounding braver than I feel.

"There is more," she admits.

"Yes?"

"Actually, Dark Crow has touched your current life. Long before either lives of this past decade occurred. His father was only half Navajo. His father's family lived in Washington, D.C."

"My hometown?"

"Indeed. On a visit, when Dark Crow was very young, his father raped and murdered a twelve-year-old girl. Dark Crow was his father's bait. He pretended to be hurt as the lure."

My entire body seems to sink. "Hannah."

Kenya nods.

"So a bear eats his dad and Puck shoots him. How appropriate." I laugh sarcastically before a peace settles over me. "I should hate him. With every bone in my body. Why don't I?"

"Superiority is born in the light, leading to hate. Compassion is born in the darkness, leading to non-violence. When we allow that we are capable of darkness ourselves, compassion is our natural response."

Like a flower unfolding, I see it. I see it all. "The black dot of yin in the white swirl of yang. The white dot of yang in the black swirl of yin. The endless questions inside of every answer. Every answer within the questioner. The time inside of

timelessness. The timelessness inside of time. The Great
Mystery an umbrella to knowing what you know. And know-
ing what you know including knowing that it is all a Great
Mystery."

"You've got it," Kenya says, smiling.

"Be sure to get that part," I tell Robin, feeling more confident than ever. I finish my story, all the way up to my daughter up there, drumming for me.

When I am finished, my biographer looks worried.

"I don't know if I can tell it like you experienced it," she
says. "It's too unreal, too fantastical, too deep. All those journeys and Dark Crow and the two Taras. Dying with Chief. The
yin and the yang. I'm not sure I can pull it off."

"Do your best," Kenya assures her. "You'll have guidance.
But remember, every detail has to be obscured. Make up things
from your own life, and the life of others you have known.
Change the location, the times, the tribes, everything. We don't
want Mary to realize herself in the story. Not for sure. She can
only be made to wonder."

"Just get the essence of it," I implore. "That is all that really
matters."

"What is the essence of it?" Robin asks, as if looking for a
direct quote.

I think for a moment, going to the place deep inside where
I know what I know. It comes to me easily. "That Faith, Hope
and Love...live."

Are You Mary?

Dear Reader:

Are you Mary? Do you know her? If I've followed my mission well, you won't know for sure. In the end, it doesn't really matter. What does matter is that there is a little of Mary in all of us. We are all needed to save our world, and to do that we must all undertake the task of saving ourselves. Fortunately, as Chief has promised, everything we need is already within us.

We at Be Who You Are Productions believe that Mary's story is so important, we have given away 1000 copies of this book. We've also made it easy for those who love the book to share it with others. The order form on the next page, and our web site at BeWhoYouAre.com, offer you the opportunity to receive our "Are You Mary?" discount when purchasing multiple copies to share with friends and family, book club members—or perfect strangers who happen upon a "forgotten" copy on an airplane or in some other random place.

You may also visit BeWhoYouAre.com for information to help you realize your own dreams. You can use our One-Step E-Mail to send a friend a short paragraph about *A Hundred Ways To Sunday*. You can also discover my Top Ten Tips To Be Who You Are, print out suggested Book Club Discussion Questions, read a portion of my next novel, submit a review for posting and more.

Be Who You Are Productions is a small company now. In the years to come, we plan to expand our offerings beyond books to include all media, supporting the work of others who offer the "Be Who You Are" message. In the meantime, practice random acts of kindness in any way Spirit moves you. Our world will be a better place for it, and your generosity will surely return to you A Hundred Ways....

All Blessings,

Robin Rice

ORDER FORM
Be Who You Are Productions

BE
WHO
YOU
ARE

Yes! Please Send Me:

1   Copy of *A Hundred Ways To Sunday* $ _13.95_

_____   Additional Copies @ the "Are You Mary?"
       discount of $10 each $_____

(Maryland Residents Add 5% Sales Tax) $_____
Add Priority Shipping of $4.50
for the first book $ _4.50_

Add $1 for each additional book $_____
TOTAL ENCLOSED $_____

A percentage of each book ordered through Be Who You Are Productions
will be donated to the Pollution Offset Lease for Earth (POLE) program
sponsored through the Dreamchange Coalition. This donation will help
"buy back" the trees used to create this book and support shamans in the Amazon.
To find out more, go to www.Dreamchange.org.

Ship To:
Name _____

Address _____

City _____

State _____ Zip _____

Telephone (_____) _____

E-mail _____

(Be assured your e-mail will never be shared or sold.)

Payment:
❑ Check sent to: Be Who You Are Productions
                 P.O. Box 57, Riva, MD 21140
❑ Credit Card: ❑ Visa   ❑ MasterCard

Card Number:_____

Name On Card: _____

Exp. Date: _____

Thank You For Your Support of Be Who You Are Productions!